GROWING UP HEALTHY

Our Illnesses

by

Robert E. Rothenberg, M.D., F.A.C.S.

A Medbook Publication

THE DANBURY PRESS

THE DANBURY PRESS
A Division of Grolier Enterprises Inc.

Robert B. Clarke, Publisher

Library of Congress Catalog Card Number: 75-29803
ISBN Number: 0-7172-8106-X

Original four volume concept by Vincent H. Jefferds

Graphix Associated   —   Production Supervision

Printed in the United States of America

2345678998

CONTENTS

A NOTE TO PARENTS

The curiosity of children is deep and limitless. They want to know everything about themselves and the world in which they live. Not too long after they have learned how to communicate, they ask, "Who made me?"—"How did I get into your tummy?"—"How did I come out?" Given another year or two and their interests begin to extend beyond the mere confines of the earthly planet on which they exist. They want to know about the stars and the sun and the moon, about God, and about life and death.

The main thesis of GROWING UP HEALTHY is that a Child's Bill of Rights is justified and is long overdue. Children are entitled to know the truth about their physical and emotional development, about their organs and how they work, about illnesses that might befall them, and about their World and Universe.

In doses sufficient to satisfy a five to ten year old's inquisitiveness and ability to comprehend, we have dispensed medical information and advice on how to maintain good health. It is our belief that the wonderful Disney characters have not only created great visual pleasure in these pages but have contributed tremendously to the enjoyment and understanding of the text.

R.E.R.

Signs of Illness

People with high fever develop great thirst.

It doesn't take a mother very long to discover when one of her youngsters feels sick. She can usually spot trouble in the time it takes to wink an eyelid. She can sense that something is wrong by the way her child looks at her, or gets out of bed, or talks or walks. Mothers are pretty smart people when it comes to knowing their children.

There are certain signs that a child doesn't feel well, and most boys and girls, when sick, will show one or more of them:

Fever

The normal temperature is 98.6° Fahrenheit. When a youngster is ill, the temperature often goes up as high as 101 or 102 or 103 or 104, or even more degrees. One can tell exactly how much fever there is by placing a thermometer in a child's mouth or rectum. However, mothers can frequently tell about temperature merely by putting their cheek against their child's cheek. If it feels hot, she will know immediately that there is a fever.

11

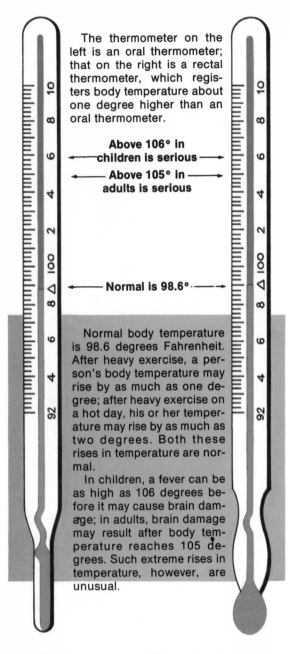

The thermometer on the left is an oral thermometer; that on the right is a rectal thermometer, which registers body temperature about one degree higher than an oral thermometer.

Above 106° in children is serious

Above 105° in adults is serious

Normal is 98.6°

Normal body temperature is 98.6 degrees Fahrenheit. After heavy exercise, a person's body temperature may rise by as much as one degree; after heavy exercise on a hot day, his or her temperature may rise by as much as two degrees. Both these rises in temperature are normal.

In children, a fever can be as high as 106 degrees before it may cause brain damage; in adults, brain damage may result after body temperature reaches 105 degrees. Such extreme rises in temperature, however, are unusual.

Fever during an illness is usually a good sign because it shows that the body is getting ready to fight the infection. With fever, a sick person breathes faster and therefore gets more oxygen into the bloodstream. With fever, the heart beats faster, and this gets more blood to the tissues. And blood contains the white blood cells that fight and overcome infections. When the temperature is high, various glands, such as the adrenal glands above the kidneys, secrete more hormones, such as adrenalin. And these hormones help us to fight infections better, too.

Slight infections may cause no increase in temperature or may only cause an increase of one or two degrees. And a minor infection with a slight fever usually lasts only a day or two. Temperatures above 101°F. indicate a somewhat more serious infection, and when a mother notes such a temperature rise, she will insist that her sick child rest in bed. Even when the temperature returns to normal and the infection clears up, a child should stay indoors for an extra day just to be sure the infection is fully controlled.

People with high fever develop great thirst. This is because they perspire a lot when their temperature is high, and the perspiration causes them to lose a great deal of fluid through their skin. For this reason, doctors always tell patients with high fever to drink a lot of fluids to replace what they have lost through sweating.

As a general rule, young children run higher temperatures than older children. When it gets too high, it can usually be brought down by giving such medicines as aspirin or by giving an antibiotic like penicillin. There are other methods, too, of bringing down a high temperature. Some of these are:

1. Giving a cool sponge bath, some-

Doctors can tell what sickness a child has because each illness has its own particular sign.

times using a little rubbing alcohol.

2. Placing the child in a tub of cold water.

3. Giving an enema containing cool water.

4. Getting the child to drink a large amount of cold liquids.

5. In hospitals, they sometimes bring down an extremely high fever by placing the patient on a specially cooled blanket. This is called a hypothermia blanket.

Fever is often higher in the afternoon and early evening than it is in the morning. Also, the temperature taken with a rectal thermometer is higher than that taken with a mouth thermometer.

Chills and chilliness

It is strange, but some children with high fever feel chilly, and occasionally have a chattering of their teeth and a shaking of their body as if they had just come out from a swim in ice-cold water. A chill, or chilly feelings, along with high fever means that the infection is pretty severe. The chill is sometimes caused by some of the germs getting into the bloodstream, or it might mean that some of the toxins (poisons) manufactured by the germs have gotten into the bloodstream.

Anyone who has a chill should be covered with warm blankets. Chills seldom last more than a few minutes. When they are over, the patient may break out in a sweat that is so big that it wets the bedsheets.

A boy or girl who has had a real chill with high temperature might just as

13

well face it. He or she will take several days before full recovery from the infection and will have to stay in bed or remain indoors for almost a week, or even more.

Sore throat

The normal throat contains large numbers of germs and viruses even when we are perfectly healthy. Many of them, like the streptococcus, the influenza and pneumonia germs, and others, could cause an illness at any time. It is strange that they don't more often than they do. Probably, it is because the child's body successfully resists these germs and keeps them from entering the membranes of the throat. Every once in a while, however, when a child's resistance is low, the germs do get into the membranes, and the throat becomes sore. In addition, the child may begin to feel sick because the toxins produced by the germs get into the blood.

A sore throat is an early sign of illness in many different diseases. It may just mean the beginning of an ordinary

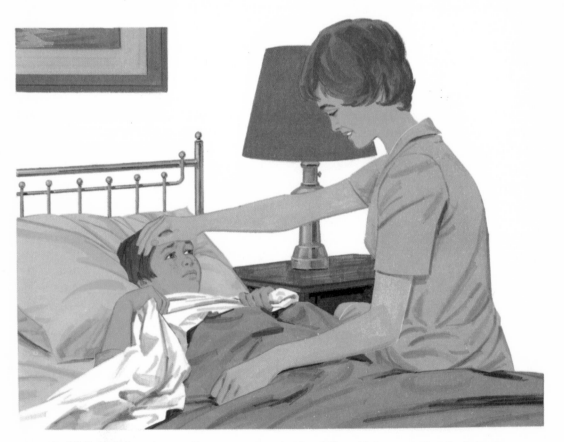

A child's high fever is sometimes accompanied by chills, which means that the infection is severe. The chills seldom last more than a few minutes.

cold or grippe or influenza. Sometimes, it means the child has caught a disease like measles or scarlet fever or mumps. Peculiarly, a day or two after the disease takes hold, the sore throat disappears.

Headache

Isn't it curious that some children never get a headache while others get them all the time? There are about fifty different causes of headache, and many times parents and doctors are unable to learn what started a particular headache. We do know, though, that almost anything can bring on a headache if the child is the type who gets them frequently. Fortunately, most headaches disappear by themselves in an hour or two, and if they don't, ordinary antiheadache pills, like aspirin, are usually all that's needed in the way of treatment. Of course, if a headache should continue for a whole day, or overnight, even after the child has been given aspirin or some other headache medicine, then the mother will call the doctor to see what the trouble is.

Here are some of the commonest reasons for headache:

1. Nervousness and upsets, due to worry or caused by disagreements in school or at home, often bring on a headache. Such headaches are called tension headaches. They often seem to affect children who are not completely happy and content in their relations with their friends and parents and sisters and brothers. If tension headaches occur frequently, it is a good idea to find out exactly what is troubling the child. Then it is usually not too difficult to overcome the problem. When that is accomplished the headaches will tend to disappear.

2. Any infection, such as an infected tooth or sinus or throat or ear, or an illness like measles or chicken pox, or even a heavy cold, may begin with a headache. The higher the temperature, the more likely is the child to have a headache. This type of headache goes away as the child's general condition improves.

3. Eyestrain may produce a headache, especially if a child reads for a long time in poor light. Also, looking at television for too long may cause eyestrain and result in a headache.

4. Overtiredness is a frequent cause of headache. Many youngsters just don't know when to quit what they are doing and rest. As a result, they get terribly tired and develop severe headaches. It is always a good idea to follow your parents' advice when they tell you to stop playing and to rest for a while. If you don't, you may get an unnecessary headache.

5. Poor ventilation sometimes causes a headache. Often, a child lives and plays in a room without proper ventilation where the windows are closed, the radiator is on full blast, and no fresh air enters the room. Air in such a room is too hot and too dry, and that can easily result in a severe headache. It is best to allow a window to be open at least a little bit, even on a nasty, rainy, or cold day. Also, it is a good idea to see that room air is kept moist. This can be accomplished by having plenty of plants and water-containing vases in a

...LOOKS LIKE WATER ON THE KNEE !

room, or by having a machine known as a humidifier in the room working to supply moisture to the air.

6. Some boys and girls are so busy with their schoolwork and their play-time activities that they skip breakfast or lunch, or skip their afternoon snack of milk and crackers. A child who gets too hungry may develop a headache. This kind can be easily gotten rid of if the child will remember to eat more regularly.

7. Some children like to holler and make a lot of noise, or to play the radio or television set much more loudly than is necessary. However, without being aware of it, a good many young-sters are sensitive to loud sounds and may develop a headache if it continues for any length of time.

A sore throat is an early sign of illness in many different diseases.

Eyestrain is a common cause of headache, and usually results from reading too long, or in poor light. If you put your reading aside for a time, or get proper light, you'll concentrate better.

8. It is natural for most children to move their bowels every day. However, sometimes they skip a day or two, and this might bring on a headachy feeling. This type of headache is not serious and disappears quickly once the child becomes regular again.

Migraine

Migraine is a special kind of headache that affects just one side of the head and is accompanied by nausea, and sometimes by vomiting. It is common in some families and seems to be inherited. Many doctors think that migraine is caused by an allergy. An allergy is a particular sensitivity to a substance such as a food or a medicine or the fur of an animal. If a child eats a certain food to which he is allergic, like chocolate, for example, or if he takes a medicine to which he is allergic, he may develop a migraine headache. Occasionally, migraine is brought on by a nervous upset, and of course, this kind of migraine has nothing to do with whether or not the child is allergic.

The migraine headache is very painful, and special medicines must be taken to relieve it. Many attacks last an entire day or even overnight, but they practically never last more than one day.

Pain

Pain that lasts for a few hours, or more, is a definite sign that something is wrong. We discussed earlier in this

17

When a child refuses things like hot dogs and hamburgers and ice cream, the chances are that he or she is not feeling too well.

chapter what a sore throat may mean; a pain in the abdomen that continues for several hours may mean that the child has an inflammation of the stomach or intestines or an inflamed appendix; a pain in the back or side may mean that the child has a kidney infection. And of course, we all know that pain is produced when someone strains a muscle or breaks a bone.

Everybody pays attention to a child who complains of pain because young people hate to feel sick and be kept away from the fun of school and play. Parents almost always take their chil-

dren's pain seriously and will call a doctor unless the pain goes away by itself in a short time. Do you know that once in a great while a child is foolish and will complain of pain when he really doesn't have any? If he does that too often his parents might not believe him when he actually does have a pain. And that can cause plenty of trouble, can't it?

Loss of appetite

Generally, healthy children love to eat, and most have big appetites. When a child suddenly loses the desire for

18

food and refuses things like hot dogs and hamburgers and ice cream, the chances are that he or she is not feeling too well. Loss of appetite is one of the earliest signs that a child is coming down with some kind of illness. As a matter of fact, most sicknesses that children get begin with loss of appetite.

Nausea and vomiting

Healthy boys and girls rarely feel sick to their stomachs and vomit. Nausea and vomiting are seen in a great many illnesses in children, even if the illness doesn't have anything to do with a disorder of the stomach or intestines. Of course, if a healthy child stuffs his stomach with the wrong kinds of food and eats more than he should, he can get sick to his stomach and throw up even if he is otherwise healthy.

Stuffy noses and inflamed eyes

Lots of illnesses start with a stuffy nose and inflamed eyes. Practically every contagious disease in childhood, including mumps and chicken pox and scarlet fever and measles, begins with a runny, stuffed-up nose and red, teary eyes. Also, the ordinary cold or grippe or flu starts this way, too. Because it occurs in so many different conditions, it is not often possible to tell what

The organisms that cause measles, scarlet fever, and mumps are very different in both size and shape. Nevertheless, all three of these childhood diseases begin with similar symptoms: runny, stuffed-up nose and red, teary eyes. Because these symptoms accompany so many conditions, they aren't much help in determining what disease a child has.

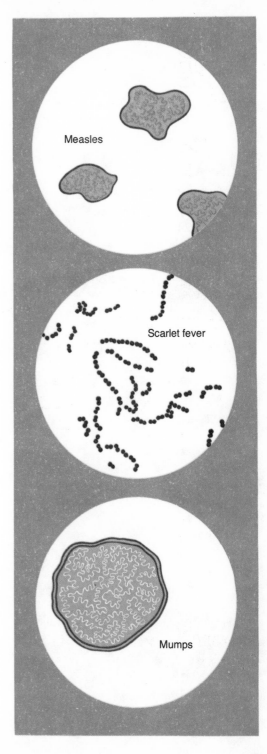

Measles

Scarlet fever

Mumps

19

sickness a child is developing merely because of a stuffy nose and inflamed eyes.

Irritability

Crankiness, lack of pep, and irritability are often early signs that a youngster is becoming ill. Mothers and fathers can frequently tell in a second that something is wrong because their child is behaving differently from his or her usual happy, cheerful, friendly self. Of course, everyone acts grumpy and sour once in a while, but when an active child with a sunny disposition suddenly becomes sad or quiet or cranky or inactive, you can bet your boots that in most instances that child is about to come down with some sort of illness. When this happens, the mother usually gets busy, and in a jiffy, she takes her child's temperature and makes an examination to find out what's behind the change in behavior.

Doctors can tell, in most cases, exactly what sickness a child is developing. It is not difficult because each illness has its own particular signs. For example, there are certain kinds of spots in the throat that appear only when the child has measles; there are certain kinds of sounds a doctor hears through a stethoscope when a child has pneumonia; and there is a certain tense, hard feel to the belly when the child has appendicitis. Of course, all young people must realize how important it is to cooperate with the doctor who is examining them. Some children, because they don't want to be sick and stay in bed, try to fool the doctor and say that they have no pain when they really do. This is silly because everyone knows that the only reason a doctor examines a child is to find out exactly what is wrong in order to know the proper medicine and treatment. And if a child doesn't tell the doctor where it hurts, and how much it hurts, it is going to be much more difficult for the doctor to make the right diagnosis and to start the right treatment.

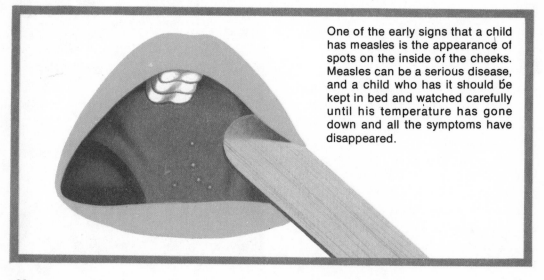

One of the early signs that a child has measles is the appearance of spots on the inside of the cheeks. Measles can be a serious disease, and a child who has it should be kept in bed and watched carefully until his temperature has gone down and all the symptoms have disappeared.

Contagious Diseases

Scarlet fever is so mild (nowadays) that children may have it without their parents' even knowing it.

When your grandparents were young, they had a pretty hard time fighting all the many contagious diseases that affected a huge number of children. There were a whole bunch of them like diphtheria, measles, German measles, mumps, whooping cough, polio, smallpox, scarlet fever, roseola and chicken pox.

Can you imagine, there are a lot of grandparents around today who had six or seven contagious diseases when they were young? And some of these diseases—especially polio, diphtheria, smallpox and scarlet fever—were very serious sicknesses. Nowadays, children are a great deal luckier because doctors have discovered vaccines that prevent most of the contagious diseases. As a matter of fact, the only diseases for which they don't have vaccines are chicken pox and roseola.

Three of the ten diseases—diphtheria, polio, and scarlet fever—used to cause a tremendous amount of trouble, but within recent years, they have become almost completely controlled. Since almost every child in this country gets diphtheria and polio vaccine, it is extremely rare to see a child with these diseases. And for some strange reason, scarlet fever has become a very mild condition, instead of the serious illness it used to be when your grandparents were children. As a matter of fact, doctors don't bother to give young boys and girls vaccinations against scarlet fever because the reaction to the vaccination will make the child sicker than scarlet fever will itself!

By the time boys and girls reach five years of age, they have received vaccinations against diphtheria, measles, German measles, whooping cough, polio, smallpox, and mumps. Therefore, there are few contagious diseases that they might get except chicken pox or scarlet fever. And, as we just mentioned, scarlet fever these days is so mild that children may have it without their parents even knowing it. They don't have to worry about roseola, either, because it almost always comes before a child is five years of age.

Chicken pox is not a serious disease, but it does seem to get around a lot. Actually, most children get chicken pox before they grow up, but if they escape it in childhood, they may catch it as adults.

Chicken pox is very contagious and spreads easily from one child to another by a sneeze or a cough, or even from touching and playing with a child who is developing chicken pox. After being with a child with chicken pox, it takes other children about two to three weeks before they get the sickness.

There is no way to stop a child who has been with a child with the disease from getting chicken pox. A lucky child might not catch it, but most times will.

Do you know how a mother tells that her child is getting chicken pox? Well, here is how it develops:

For a day or two, the child doesn't feel very well and may have a few sniffles, and it looks as if he or she is catching cold. Then, the appetite isn't very good, and some temperature may develop. On the second or third day of the illness, a few tiny spots appear on the body, mostly on the chest, abdomen, and upper part of the arms and thighs. Soon these spots form blisters, and they cover most of the head and neck and rest of the body. Within a couple of days, the drops of fluid within the blisters turn from a clear to a cloudy color. Then, after four or five days, the blisters dry up and form scabs. The scabs take a couple of weeks before they fall off. *A child should never scratch or pick off a chicken pox scab as it may cause a permanent scar.* If a blister or scab itches, a warm bath or a medicine spread over the scabs will stop the itching.

By the time all the blisters have dried up and formed scabs, the temperature is normal and the child feels perfectly all right. Also, when all the blisters are gone, the child can no longer give the disease to another child.

Boys and girls who are getting well from chicken pox are sometimes pretty unhappy because they must sit around and wait for their scabs to fall off before they can play with their friends or go back to school. Actually, it wouldn't do any harm if they did resume their activities earlier, as the disease is no longer contagious after the scabs have formed. But teachers and mothers of other children usually don't want to have children around when they're still covered with scabs.

Children who have recovered from chicken pox should know that almost all of the marks left by the scabs will disappear in time. It is only when a scab has become infected from picking and scratching that it may leave a scar.

Although it may be difficult to believe, there are still many poor and undeveloped parts of the world where children are unable to get shots and vaccinations to prevent contagious diseases. As a result, epidemics do take place from time to time. Here are some of the diseases these unfortunate children may catch:

Diphtheria

This is a disease in which there is fever and a severe sore throat. It is caused by the diphtheria germ, and if the condition is not treated quickly, it may cause heart trouble or paralysis of nerves. Even when the disease is brought under control, it takes several weeks to recover.

Measles

It takes a week or two to catch measles from another child. It starts out like an ordinary cold, with a stuffy nose and runny eyes, but then the child develops fever, a dry cough, and a rash all over the body. The rash lasts about a week, but it takes two or three weeks before the patient fully recovers. When measles is very severe, it may affect the kidneys or other important organs.

You get measles only once.

The pain of mumps is often made worse when the child eats spicy foods.

Contagious Diseases of Childhood

Disease	At what age is a child most likely to get it?	How is the disease transmitted?	How long before he gets sick?
Smallpox *Cause: smallpox or variola virus*	At any age	Direct or indirect contact with throat or skin discharges of patient and airborne spread	7 to 16 days
Poliomyelitis *Cause: 3 types of polio virus*	At any age, but most common among infants and children	Fecal contamination or direct or indirect contact with nose or throat discharges of patient	3 to 28 days, usually 7 to 12
Diphtheria *Cause: diphtheria bacteria*	Usually 1 to 14 years	Direct contact with nose or throat discharges of a carrier or patient	1 to 6 days
Whooping cough *Cause: pertussis bacteria*	Birth to 8 years	Direct contact with nose or throat discharges of a carrier or patient	5 to 16 days, usually 7 to 10
Measles *Cause: rubeola virus*	2 to 8 years	Direct or indirect contact with nose or throat discharges of patient and airborne spread	7 to 14 days, usually 10 to 12
German measles *Cause: rubella virus*	2 to 15 years	Direct or indirect contact with nose or throat discharges of patient and airborne spread	10 to 28 days, usually 14 to 21
Chickenpox *Cause: varicella virus*	2 to 8 years	Discharges from skin lesions or from nose or throat of patient and airborne spread	10 to 21 days, usually 14 to 16
Mumps *Cause: mumps virus*	Usually 2 to 14 years	Direct or indirect contact with nose or throat discharges of patient	12 to 28 days, usually 16 to 20
Influenza *Cause: influenza viruses*	As new strains develop, at any age	Direct or indirect contact with nose or throat discharges of patient. Possibly airborne spread	1 to 2 days
Scarlet fever or scarlatina *Cause: 46 types of streptococcal bacteria*	1 to 9 years	Direct or indirect contact with patient or (usually) a carrier	1 to 5 days
Infectious hepatitis *Cause: probably a virus*	At any age	Fecal contamination, contact with patient or contaminated water or food	2 to 7 weeks, usually 3 to 4 weeks
Infectious mononucleosis *Cause: unknown, believed to be a virus*	2 to 14 years	Unknown. Believed to be direct contact or from nose and throat discharges of patient	Unknown, believed to be 2 to 6 weeks
Roseola *Cause: unknown, believed to be a virus*	6 months to 3 years	Unknown. Probably direct or indirect contact with nose and throat discharges of infected patient or airborne spread	Unknown, believed to be 10 to 15 days
Acute Diarrheal diseases *Cause: many viruses, bacteria and other organisms*	At any age, most common from birth to 5 years	Direct contact, fecal contamination	Variable, usually 2 to 4 days
Bacterial meningitis *Several types*	At any age, younger children more susceptible	Direct or indirect contact with patient	Variable

What are the early signs of illness?	How long will he be sick?	How long is it contagious?	Are there permanent aftereffects?	Can he catch it again?
High fever, prostration, characteristic eruption	1 to 7 weeks	4 to 5 days before rash, until scabs disappear	1% to 40% of cases may die; blindness, brain damage, pox scars may occur	Rarely
Fever, headache, sore throat, nausea, vomiting, muscle pain and weakness	Highly variable, possibly several months	Variable from 1 week before to 3 months after onset, usually from 3 days before to 10 days after onset	Death (5% to 10% of paralytic cases) Residual paralysis may be permanent	Yes, a different type
Mild fever, sore throat, running nose	Highly variable, possibly several weeks	Variable, usually from 3 days before to 10 days after onset	5% to 10% of cases die. Possible heart or nervous system damage	Yes
Cold, with a gradually increasing dry, intermittent cough, especially at night	2 to 10 weeks, usually 4 to 6 weeks	Variable, usually first 2 weeks	In infants, death and brain damage	Mild infection may recur in adulthood
Gradually increasing fever, cold, severe cough, conjunctivitis, running nose	6 to 12 days	4 days before to end of rash	Occasionally death and brain damage	Unlikely
Slight fever, swelling of lymph glands, rash	1 to 4 days	1 week before to end of rash	Rarely, except for damage to the fetus early in pregnancy	Unlikely
Slight fever, characteristic eruption	9 to 14 days	1 day before until skin lesions scab	Rarely	Very unlikely
Fever, swelling of salivary glands (posterior part of the jaw)	4 to 10 days	1 week before to end of swelling	Very rarely brain damage	Rarely
Sudden fever, marked prostration, dry cough, muscular pain	3 to 10 days	1 day before to 4 days after onset	Very rarely	Yes
Fever, sore throat, nausea, vomiting	4 to 10 days	Highly variable. Possibly several months, usually 1 to 2 weeks	Kidney disease or rheumatic heart disease	No
Fever, mild headache, chilliness, fatigue, jaundice	Variable, 2 to 4 weeks	Unknown, believed to be approximately 3 weeks before onset until 1 week after onset of symptoms	Rarely death and chronic liver disease	Rarely
Fever, sore throat, fatigue, possibly rash, enlarged lymph nodes	Highly variable, 1 week to several months	Unknown, presumably several days before until end of sore throat	Rarely	Unknown, believed to be unlikely
High fever for 3 to 5 days. Rash occurs after temperature returns to normal	4 to 6 days	Unknown	Rarely	Unlikely
Fever, nausea, vomiting, abdominal pain, prostration	Variable, usually 2 to 5 days	Occasionally for months, usually shortly before onset until 5 days after onset	Variable	Yes
Fever, headache, irritability, nausea, muscular rigidity	Variable, usually 1 to 3 weeks	Variable, probably less than 1 day after the beginning of proper treatment	Brain damage is frequent; 10% of cases may die	Yes

25

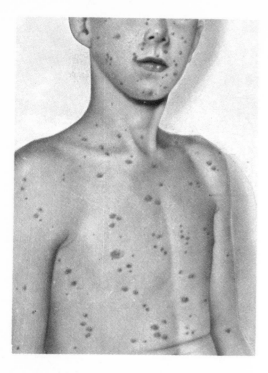

Typical chicken pox rash. Chicken pox is by no means a dangerous disease, but it can often cause disfiguring scars if the child is permitted to pick at the scabs. It is important to keep the child's fingernails clipped, and he should be urged not to scratch the pockmarks.

German measles

German measles is a completely different disease than measles because it is caused by a different virus. It takes two to three weeks to develop, and its first signs are a slight fever, a mild cold, and swelling of the glands in the back of the neck. Within a day or two, a light pinkish rash comes all over the body. A child with German measles doesn't feel terribly sick and is usually better in four to five days.

The real danger of German measles is when a pregnant woman catches the condition. If she does, it is possible that her unborn child may be affected. For this reason, every young girl should be vaccinated against German measles before she gets married.

You get German measles only once.

Mumps

Mumps is an inflammation of the glands at the angle of the jaws. It is caused by a virus that spreads from one person to another through coughing, or sometimes from kissing someone who is getting mumps. It usually takes two to three weeks for mumps to develop after one has been exposed to a person with the illness.

Children with mumps have fever and a painful swelling on the side of the face beneath the ears. Mumps is an inflammation of the parotid gland which secretes saliva. The pain is often made worse when the patient eats spicy foods.

The swelling of the glands lasts anywhere from five to ten days and then goes away. It is a good idea for children to get mumps vaccine to prevent mumps. In boys and girls over twelve years of age, and in grown-ups, mumps sometimes causes a serious, painful inflammation of the testicles or ovaries. And so, if the condition can be avoided by vaccination, such inflammation will not take place.

Once in a great while, a child will have mumps on one side only, and then, years later, may have mumps on the opposite side.

Whooping cough

Whooping cough is passed from one

person to another by coughing. It usually takes one week to a week and a half to catch the condition.

The disease starts out like an ordinary cold, but the child then begins to cough more and more often, with the worst coughing taking place at night. The coughing, once it starts, is hard for the patient to stop. As a matter of fact, children with whooping cough lose their breath, and at the end of a fit of coughing, they breathe in a huge amount of air in a sudden gulp. When they do that, they make a loud sound like a "whoop." That is how the disease got its name.

Whooping cough lasts a long time, anywhere from four to six weeks. Even after that time, a child may continue to cough every once in a while for a few more weeks.

To prevent whooping cough, all children should be given the whooping cough vaccine. And they should take booster shots if a friend or member of the family should get the condition.

Once in a while, a grown-up who had whooping cough as a child may get a

Most children get chicken pox before they grow up, but if they escape it in childhood, they may catch it as adults.

mild attack if he is exposed to the disease again.

Polio

Polio used to cripple more children than any other disease, but, fortunately, we have practically done away with the condition by giving polio vaccine. All children should get the vaccine when they're just babies, and they should get booster doses at various times when they are older.

Polio takes about one to two weeks to catch. It starts with headache, sore throat, fever, vomiting, and pains in the muscles of the arms or legs. Within a couple of days, weakness of the muscles may be so severe that the child is unable to move an arm or leg, or even both arms and legs. If the weakness, or paralysis, of one or more of the limbs doesn't clear up within a few days, it may be permanent. Isn't it wonderful that we have practically conquered this terrible disease? And isn't it a shame that every single child in the whole world isn't given polio vaccine?

Smallpox

Smallpox is one of the most contagious of all diseases, and hundreds of years ago it would affect millions of people at the same time. Nowadays smallpox has been controlled by vaccination. It is so well controlled in most

Children with whooping cough lose their breath at the end of a fit of coughing, so they breathe in a big gulp of air. When they do that, they make a sound like a "whoop"! That's how the disease got its name.

NORMAL VACCINATION REACTIONS showing typical "take"

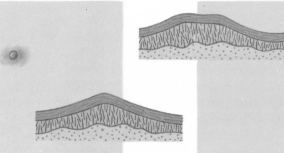

4th Day—showing hard, red, round, raised area

6th Day—showing pearly blister surrounded by red area

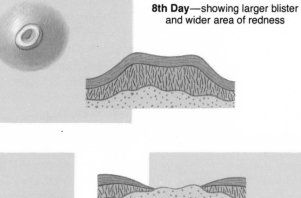

8th Day—showing larger blister and wider area of redness

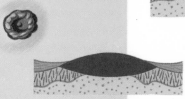

12th Day—showing dried blister which has formed a brownish scab

24th Day—showing scar of vaccination which is beginning to turn white

Smallpox vaccination reactions. It is a common misconception that only young children need to be vaccinated against smallpox. Before traveling to areas where smallpox exists, it is wise to be re-vaccinated. Many adults will have positive reactions if they have not been vaccinated for many years.

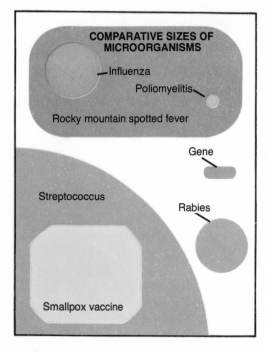

COMPARATIVE SIZES OF MICROORGANISMS

Influenza

Poliomyelitis

Rocky mountain spotted fever

Gene

Streptococcus

Rabies

Smallpox vaccine

The streptococcus organism is so small that 780,000 would fit on the head of a pin. The polio virus is 20 times smaller than the streptococcus germ.

countries that cases seldom appear and, as a result, some doctors have stopped giving smallpox vaccinations. It takes one to two weeks to catch smallpox. The disease starts with a high fever, and the patients feel extremely weak. They then break out in a rash that looks very much like chicken pox, except that there are many more pock marks and one blister may be located right next to another. Instead of the patients getting well in a few days, as they do with chicken pox, they get sicker for about a week.

Smallpox is a very serious disease and often damages the eyes or the brain. Unfortunately, the scabs don't heal nicely, as they do in chicken pox, and patients who have recovered from smallpox usually have scars that will remain permanently.

People get smallpox once only.

Scarlet fever

Scarlet fever is caused by a type of streptococcus germ that is much weaker than it used to be many years ago. In those days, a child with scarlet fever would have a very high fever, an extremely sore throat, nausea and vomiting, and would break out in a scarlet rash covering almost the entire body. Peculiarly, the skin around the mouth was not affected by the rash, and a child would therefore look as if there were a ring around the lips.

The child remained very sick for about a week. After that, the temperature would come down to normal and the rash would begin to fade. Then the skin would begin to flake and to peel. Sometimes it would look as if the child had dandruff all over his body.

Severe cases of scarlet fever used to damage the heart and sometimes the kidneys.

As we mentioned before, scarlet fever today is so mild that a child might have a fever for only a day or two, a slight sore throat, and a light rash. No peeling results, and the child feels fine about two to three days after first taking sick.

There is a vaccination against scarlet fever, but doctors don't use it because it makes children sicker than the condition itself.

Roseola

This disease only affects infants and children under four years of age.

We are very lucky because we can correct nearsightedness and farsightedness very easily with glasses.

NEW!

Nearsightedness and Farsightedness

Some people have big ears, others have small ones; some people have long noses, others have short ones. And of course, some folks have ears and noses that are just about medium. But did you know that some people, including children, have "long eyeballs," while others have "short eyeballs"? When the eyeball is longer than normal instead of being round in shape, people are nearsighted, and when their eyeballs are shorter than normal, they are farsighted. In other words, a nearsighted person has an eyeball that is a little bit egg-shaped, while a farsighted person has an eyeball that is flatter than the round shape of the perfect eyeball. Look at the drawings on page 32 and you will see the differences between the shapes of the normal eyeball, the nearsighted eyeball, and the farsighted eyeball.

The eye is very much like a camera. The round, black part in the center of the eye is called the pupil. It gets bigger in the dark to let more light into the eye, and it gets smaller in a bright light. The diaphragm of a camera works the same way. It is regulated so that the opening is larger in dim light and smaller in bright light.

The colored portion of the eye is called the iris and it is composed of a muscle that contracts and relaxes. When the iris muscle contracts, the pupil gets smaller; and when it relaxes, the pupil gets larger. You can see that for yourself very easily. Turn off the light in your room, so it is not very bright. Next, hold a flashlight in your hand or, if you don't have a flashlight, hold your hand on the chain of a lamp. Now, ask your mother to sit close to you so you can stare into her eyes. Finally, flash the light into her eyes—or pull the chain on the lamp—and as you look into her eyes, you will see her pupil immediately get smaller.

Just like a camera, the eye has a lens through which the light passes. The purpose of the lens is to focus the light on the retina in the back of the eye. When it is focused properly, we see things clearly; when it doesn't focus properly, things look all blurred and unclear. Doctors always compare the retina of the eye to the film in a camera. It is the place where the light finally strikes and is turned into something we can see.

In a nearsighted person, since the eyeball is too long, the light focuses in front of the retina, and in a farsighted person, because the eyeball is too short, the light focuses beyond the retina. As a result, nearsighted and farsighted people can't see as clearly as those with perfectly shaped eyeballs. However, we are pretty lucky because we can correct nearsightedness and farsightedness very easily with eyeglasses. All we have to do is to have our eyes tested by an eye doctor and, in a jiffy, he can tell us exactly what kind of glasses we need to make our sight normal.

Most children don't have to wear their eyeglasses all the time even if they are nearsighted or farsighted. A great many boys and girls will need the glasses only when they read, or watch television, or go to the movies. And nearsighted and farsighted youngsters can use their eyes just as much as those who don't wear glasses. Eyes are not weak just because they require eye-glasses!

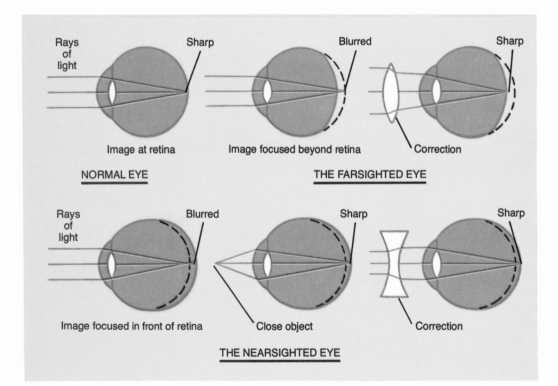

NORMAL EYE   THE FARSIGHTED EYE   THE NEARSIGHTED EYE

Wearing Eyeglasses

A child who discovers how much clearer everything looks through eyeglasses is happy to wear them.

Lots of boys and girls wear eyeglasses to help them see better, but every once in a while, a child will complain about using them. However, a child who discovers how much clearer everything looks through eyeglasses is happy to wear them. Unfortunately, almost everybody has something that is wrong. Some children have flat feet and have to wear arches in their shoes; some kids get cavities in their teeth and must have fillings put in; and still other children have large tonsils and adenoids which must be removed to improve their health. And so, it isn't so bad to wear eyeglasses. As a matter of fact, if you look around the next time you go out on the street, you'll find out that almost half the people are wearing glasses.

Children who wear glasses should take good care of them. They should realize that eyeglasses are expensive, so they must try not to break them. Here are a few good things to know about eyeglasses:

1. Be sure not to throw your glasses around. Even the strongest ones can break if they are treated too roughly.

2. Eyeglass frames can break or bend

out of shape if you put them in your pants pocket when not wearing them. Accidentally, you might sit or fall on them. Put your glasses in your shirt or jacket pocket when you take them off.

3. Eyeglasses are safest when you put them in their eyeglass case. The case protects them from breaking or bending. When the frames bend, the lenses may not focus the light properly on your retina and you won't see as clearly as you should.

4. Don't play rough games like football while wearing glasses, and don't wrestle or fight with your glasses on.

5. When you take off your glasses, put them down so the lenses do not lie on the table or desk where they might get scratched.

6. Wash your glasses regularly with soap and water. Dirty eyeglasses may blur your vision or strain your eyes needlessly.

7. Tell your parents if you think you are not seeing clearly through your glasses. You may need another checkup with the eye doctor.

8. Make sure your name and address are written clearly inside the eyeglass case. Then, if you are careless and lose them, some nice person may return them to you.

Wash your glasses regularly with soap and water.

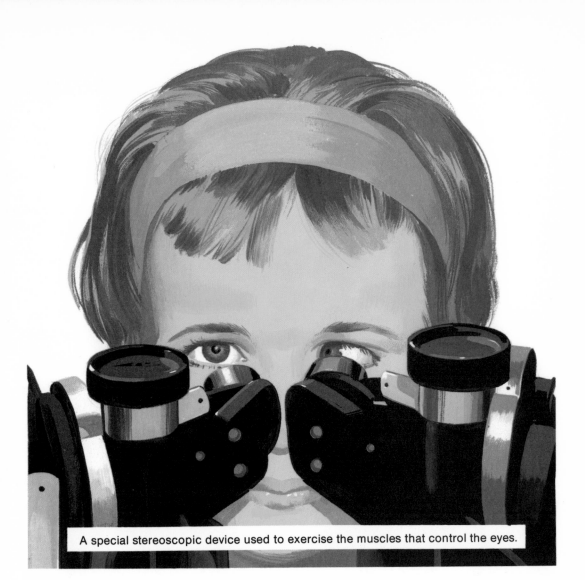

A special stereoscopic device used to exercise the muscles that control the eyes.

Crossed Eyes

Newborn babies often look as if their eyes are crossed. This is because it takes them a few weeks to learn how to make both their eyes work together properly. Once in a while, a child's eyes don't straighten out and they remain permanently crossed.

Having crossed eyes usually doesn't mean that anything is wrong with the eyes themselves. The trouble is with one or more of the muscles attached to the outside of the eyeball.

All of us have ocular muscles, six around each eye, which allow us to move our eyes in all directions. For some reason or other, certain children have muscles that are either too weak or too strong. When that happens, the affected eyeball doesn't move the way it should. Instead of both eyes moving

35

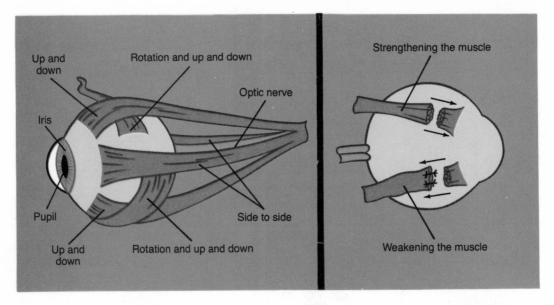

Movement and position of the eyeball are controlled by muscles at the sides and top and bottom of the sclera, or hard white shell of the eye. Crossed eyes are corrected surgically by weakening a muscle to lengthen it or shortening a muscle to strengthen it. Such operations are usually done when a child is four or five years of age.

in the same direction at the same time, the eye with the problem muscle or muscles stays in the same place or turns the wrong way. The child then looks cross-eyed.

Unfortunately, there are boys and girls who tease and make fun of a child with crossed eyes. This is a very mean thing to do, and we know you would never do it, would you? Of course not! You understand that crossed eyes are just like any other thing that may go wrong with a child that is beyond his control.

Eye doctors know how to fix crossed eyes without too much trouble. They usually do it when a child is about four to five years of age. To straighten out the eyes, it is necessary to go to the hospital for a few days and to have an operation. Luckily, it won't hurt, because the child goes to sleep before the operation, and there is very little pain after the operation is over. A bandage is placed over both eyes for a day after the operation, but then the child sees again and, in all probability, will see a lot better than he or she did before. It is only necessary to stay in the hospital for three to four days after the operation. However, a child whose eyes have been straightened should not take part in too strenuous activities—like riding a bicycle, swimming, roughhousing or things like that—for a few weeks.

Occasionally, after an operation to correct crossed eyes, a child will see double for a few weeks. However, that disappears as the child learns how to make both eyes work together.

Hearing and Deafness

As we all know, we can lose hearing temporarily if water gets into our ears while swimming.

Deafness means loss of hearing. It can affect one or both ears. Deafness may mean complete loss of hearing or only a partial loss.

Most children who are born with good hearing will grow up to hear well. Years ago, many children developed some deafness as a result of illnesses that led to ear infections. Nowadays, with the use of early treatment, including the antibiotic medicines, ear infections that would lead to deafness can be controlled before they damage hearing.

In the old days when your grandparents were young, there were many illnesses around, like measles and mumps and scarlet fever, that were sometimes followed by severe ear infections and loss of hearing. Today, thank goodness, there are vaccines to prevent measles and mumps, and antibiotics to knock out scarlet fever, so practically nobody has to fear deafness from these conditions! Unfortunately, no one has yet learned how to do away with the ordinary cold. And colds can be followed by ear infections if they are especially severe, or if they are neglected by not going to bed and taking medicines when there is a fever.

Infections of the middle ear and mastoid bones behind the ear are the commonest causes of hearing loss. Do you remember, we talked about the middle ear in the first volume of these books? The middle ear contains the eardrum and the three little bones of hearing, and the middle ear connects with the Eustachian tube which leads to the throat. Once in a while, when someone has a severe cold or sore throat or infected tonsils, the infection travels up the Eustachian tube to the middle ear. The infection sometimes travels even further and infects the mastoid bones near where the inner ear is located. Unless these middle ear and mastoid bone infections are cleared up quickly by giving large doses of antibiotic medicines, some permanent damage to hearing may result. Luckily, in most cases, hearing returns to normal after these infections clear up.

Naturally, the best way to avoid ear infections is to treat the cold or sore throat or tonsillitis *before* the infection has a chance to spread. And, of course, if a child gets repeated infections of the tonsils, the best thing to do is to have them removed. Another thing: children who have stuffed noses should not sniff up the mucus, as this may cause it to get into the Eustachian tubes. And besides, they should not blow their noses too hard to get rid of the mucus because this, too, may cause some of it to get into the Eustachian tubes.

There are a few other conditions that can lead to deafness, but, fortunately, they don't happen very often. A child can lose some hearing if he or she runs an extremely high temperature for a week or two or has an infection of the brain such as encephalitis or meningitis. Once in a while, a severe fall on the head may cause damage to the nerve of hearing, and that can cause deafness,

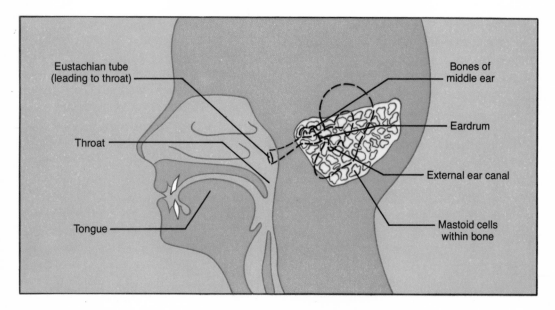

The mastoid air cells can become infected by an extension of the inflammation from the middle ear. When they do, antibiotics are given to control the infection. Sometimes it requires surgery to get rid of the infection by scraping and draining the mastoid cells.

While some kinds of deafness are permanent, others last only a short time.

too. And, as we have mentioned elsewhere in these books, occasionally a child is born deaf. In such cases, the deafness is usually permanent. However, some day doctors may discover a way to restore hearing to children who are born deaf.

In addition to the kinds of deafness that are permanent, there are several types that last only a short time. For example, wax can collect in the ear canals and can be so heavily packed in the canal that it interferes with hearing. Loss of hearing can also result when children put something into their ears, like a marble or a bean or a bead or a pebble. And, as we all know, we can lose hearing temporarily when we get water into our ears when swimming.

Teachers and parents sometimes complain that a child doesn't seem to hear normally. In most instances, it is not due to real deafness. The lack of hearing in these children comes about because they don't pay attention to what is being said to them. Actually, no one hears well unless he pays attention.

Would you like to try an experiment? If you are reading this book, you are not paying attention to all the sounds coming from outside. Put the book down, or if someone is reading to you, ask them to put down the book. Now, listen quietly to all the sounds you weren't hearing while you were reading or being read to. The same sounds were there all the time, but you didn't hear them because you weren't paying attention. That's why your mother gets so angry when she calls and calls you, and you don't answer. In all probability, you were concentrating so much on a TV or radio program that you didn't hear her calling.

We hear everything much better when we look at the person who is speaking to us. Without knowing it, we watch their lips move as they speak, and this helps to hear and understand what they are saying even if they are talking in a quiet whisper. In other words, our eyes help our ears to work better. If you want to prove this, have someone talk to you very softly while he covers his mouth with his hand. You may not hear what he is saying. Then, ask him to say the same thing again in the same soft tone but not while covering his mouth with his hand. See how much more clearly you hear him?

People with hearing loss can use their eyes to help themselves, too. They to an infection of the inner or middle ear can often be helped greatly by using a hearing aid. These are little gadgets that make things sound louder in much the same way as a loudspeaker in a radio or television set makes sounds louder. Hearing aids use a tiny electric battery that is no bigger than the tip of

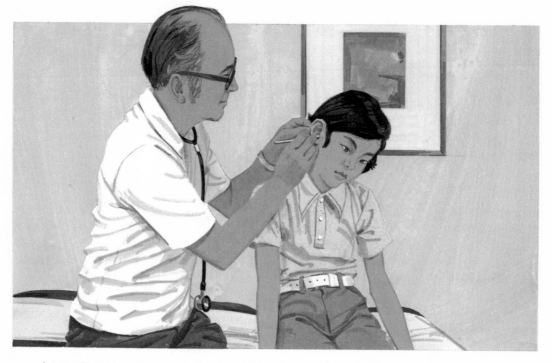

Loss of hearing can result when a child puts something in his ear, like a bean or a pebble. Such foreign bodies can be removed from the ear with a small forceps, but this should only be done by a physician.

can be taught how to understand what others are saying by lip reading. There are courses given in special schools for the deaf that teach how to read lips, and it is amazing how quickly a person with hearing loss can learn it. Actually, deaf people who read lips are hearing with their eyes!

Children who have lost hearing due a finger. A hearing aid is fitted snugly into the ear canal and is made so cleverly that it is hardly noticeable. Of course, if a boy or girl wears long hair, it can't be seen at all. Hearing aids can be worn all day long and will not fall out while a child is running or playing. Naturally, we take them out of our ears when we go in the water.

Wax in the Ears

The part of the ear that sticks out from the side of the head is not the really important part of the ear. It is called the external ear, and it merely catches sounds and directs them into the ear canal. From there, the sound waves pass through the eardrum into the middle ear where hearing actually starts to take place.

Did you know that a person can hear almost as well as normal even without the part of the ear that sticks out from the side of the head? Well, it's true. Take Donald Duck, as an example; he doesn't have ears sticking out from his head, yet he hears very well indeed.

The ear canal is curvy, and that helps to protect the eardrum from anything that might accidentally get into the ear. Also, the skin that lines the ear canal manufactures an orange-colored, sticky wax that prevents tiny insects or dust from getting near the eardrum. An insect's feet will get caught in the sticky wax, so he won't be able to get very far inside. Dust and dirt that might fly into the ear from a gust of wind also get stopped by the sticky wax. This system of protection works

A big collection of hard wax in the ear canal can interfere with hearing.

beautifully. Just think, you never heard of anyone getting a mosquito bite deep inside the ear, did you?

Some children have the bad habit of sticking things into their ears, and it is possible that they could scratch or injure the skin that lines the ear canal. So, everyone is taught not to put pencils, sticks, or other pointy things into their ears.

Once in a while, the glands in the skin of the ear canals make more wax than is actually needed. Then, the wax collects in the canal and from time to time, pieces of the wax fall out of the canal. Occasionally, the wax hardens in the canal and it doesn't fall out as it should. As a matter of fact, a big collection of hard wax in the ear canal can interfere with hearing.

Excess wax in the ear canal can usually be wiped out with a bit of cotton, but a child should not try to do this alone. Most times, a mother or father will take a cotton applicator and will remove it easily. Sometimes, though, there is so much wax, and the wax is so hard, that even a mother or father can't get it out. In such cases, the child is taken to a doctor who will remove it without much trouble. The doctor may first have the child use some eardrops to soften the wax so it will come out easily in a day or two. Or, the doctor might take a syringe and fill it with warm water and then syringe out the wax. It doesn't hurt to remove wax from the ear, although it might feel a bit uncomfortable for a short time. But it is amazing how much better a person hears after getting rid of a lot of ear wax.

The skin that lines the ear canal manufactures a sticky wax that prevents tiny insects or dust from getting near the eardrum, and protects the ear's delicate hearing mechanism. Once in a while, the wax can build up and harden into a plug that interferes with hearing. Then it must be removed by a physician.

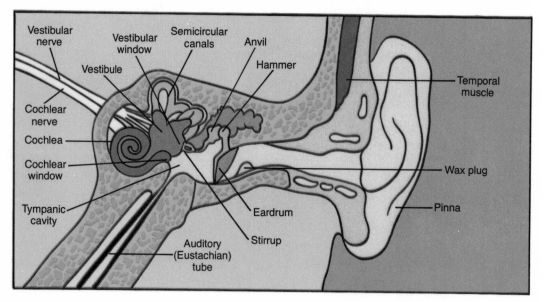

Tonsils and Adenoids

Just think how great it will be to get rid of those awful sore throats and how good it will feel to breathe easily through the nose.

Until just a few years ago, almost all children had their tonsils and adenoids removed before they reached five or six years of age. That was because the tonsils and adenoids would become infected so often and would cause frequent colds, sore throats, and high fever. We are much luckier today than we used to be because wonderful new medicines like penicillin and other antibiotics are able to cure tonsil and adenoid infections before a child really gets very sick. As a result, many children nowadays don't need to have their tonsils and adenoids removed.

Unfortunately, some youngsters get infections of the tonsils and adenoids over and over again, even though they are given penicillin or some other medicine like it. These children are much better off if they go to the hospital for a day or two and have their tonsils and

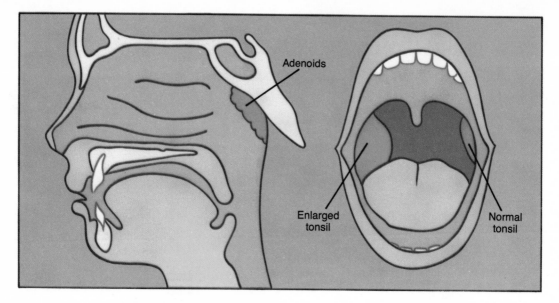

On the right, one tonsil is of normal size and the other one is enlarged because of infection. On the left, the enlarged adenoids are shown. These glandlike organs are believed to localize and give immunity to some respiratory infections. However, when they are chronically enlarged they should be removed.

adenoids removed. Then, they can't ever get infected again!

Everyone has two tonsils, located in the back of the throat, one on each side just back of the tongue. They are about the size and shape of a large green olive, but when they become infected— wow!—they can be swollen almost to the size of a plum.

The adenoids are hidden high up behind the throat near the back of the nose. When they become infected and enlarged, they often make it difficult for a child to breathe through the nose. You have seen little girls or boys, haven't you, who always have their mouths open and seem to have a sort of dumb look on their faces? Well, they aren't really dumb or stupid; they just look that way because their adenoids are swollen and block air that ordina-

rily passes out of the back of the nose and goes down into the windpipe in the neck. In order to get enough air into their lungs, children with large adenoids breathe through their mouths.

The tonsils and the adenoids are removed at the same time so that the two problems—frequent sore throats and mouth breathing—are both solved by the one simple operation. Fortunately, removal of the tonsils and adenoids is not very serious and doesn't cause too much pain or discomfort. Oh, the throat is usually sore for a couple of days after the operation, and it is necessary to stay indoors for a few days after coming home from the hospital. But just think how great it will be to get rid of those awful sore throats, and how good it will feel to breathe easily through the nose!

Swollen Glands

Lymph glands, or, as doctors call them "lymph nodes" are bean-sized structures that are present in various places in our bodies. Although these nodes are present in lots of places, they can be felt most easily in the neck, under the arms, and in the groin where the main part of the body joins the thighs.

Lymph glands are connected to lymph channels, which are tiny hollow tubes through which the whitish fluid called lymph flows. Lymph travels through the lymph channels in much the same way as blood flows through the arteries and veins of the body. When an infection takes place and is strong enough to spread from the site where it first started, the germs or their poisons travel through the lymph channels until they reach the lymph glands. Each lymph gland is composed of millions of white blood cells that fight off the germs or the poisons the germs manufacture. In most cases, the lymph glands are successful in controlling the germs and their poisons, and are able to prevent them from reaching the bloodstream. In this way, they prevent the infection from traveling to other parts of the body.

Lymph glands do not have an easy job in fighting and winning over germs or poisons. And during the fight to control the infection, a lymph gland may become very swollen and painful to the touch. For example, when we have a severe sore throat or inflammation of the tonsils, the lymph glands in the neck become painful and swollen. If there is a severe infection of a toe, the lymph glands in the groin may get large and tender. Or, if there is an infected finger, the lymph glands in the armpit may swell and become painful.

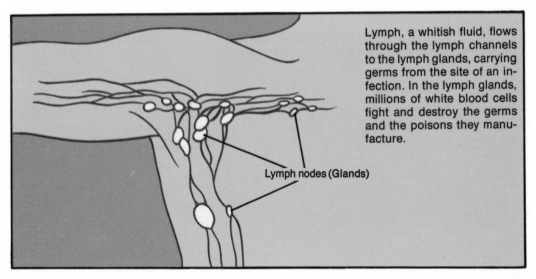

Lymph, a whitish fluid, flows through the lymph channels to the lymph glands, carrying germs from the site of an infection. In the lymph glands, millions of white blood cells fight and destroy the germs and the poisons they manufacture.

Lymph nodes (Glands)

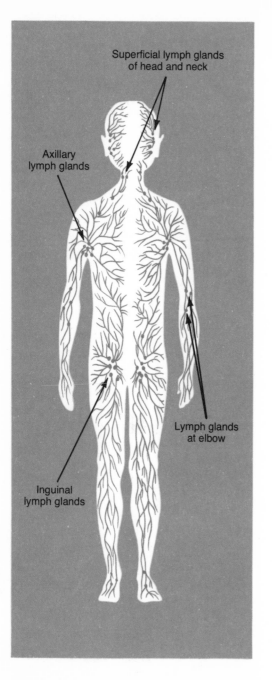

The superficial lymph channels and lymph glands (nodes) lie beneath the skin and subcutaneous tissues. The white blood cells in the lymph glands combat infections and prevent their spread to other parts of the body.

One of the first things a doctor does when examining someone with an infection is to feel the lymph glands. If they are swollen and tender, the doctor knows that a pretty severe infection is present. Usually, the patient will be told to take antibiotic medicines to help the lymph glands stop the infection from traveling farther to other parts of the body. The patient will also have to rest in bed and drink large amounts of water and other liquids. Doing these things also helps to overcome an infection.

Fortunately, rest in bed, warm moist soaks to the infected area, drinking lots of fluids, and taking the wonderful antibiotic medicines is enough to knock out most infections, and within a few days, or at most a couple of weeks, the lymph glands return to their normal size and lose their pain and tenderness. Once in a great while, however, the infection is so powerful that it causes an abscess to form in a lymph gland. When this happens, the doctor will have to cut into the gland in order to let the pus drain out.

When the lymph glands are exceptionally painful, warm, wet soaks often relieve the discomfort. Such soaks can be applied by wetting a washcloth or towel. And if the pain is very strong, the doctor may recommend that the patient take a pain-relieving medicine, such as aspirin.

Everyone should be thankful that the body has plenty of lymph glands spread throughout it. Without them, germs and their poisons would have a much easier time going from place to place in our bodies.

Sore Throat

Sore throats due to any kind of allergy can be helped by avoiding the irritating pollen or other substances that are in the air.

Sore throats are a real pain in the neck, aren't they? But I guess we ought to be glad we're not an ostrich or a giraffe. Can you imagine how they must feel with a sore throat?

Nothing makes a child crankier than a throat that hurts when swallowing or talking, or just when doing nothing. And, unfortunately, boys and girls seem to get sore throats much more often than grown-ups do.

There are lots of reasons for sore throats; some we can control, others we can't do much about.

The commonest reason for a sore throat is that we are about to catch a cold. The soreness usually begins the day before our nose gets stuffed up and begins to run. We *can* do something to prevent this kind of sore throat. Do you know what? We can do all the things we're supposed to do to prevent colds, such as wearing rubbers or boots when going out in the rain, wearing a jacket or coat when it's chilly, and staying away from other children who already have colds. Then, if we don't catch the cold, our throats won't be sore.

Some sore throats are caused by a different kind of germ than the one that causes a cold. These sore throats may be caused by a streptococcus germ, and that can make a child pretty sick. There isn't much anyone can do to avoid this type of sore throat, except to stay away from a child who already has the condition.

Years ago, when your mom and dad were young, it was serious to get a streptococcus sore throat, and often people with this sickness would have to go to the hospital. Nowadays, the wonderful antibiotic medicines clear up a "strep throat" in a very short time. Of course, children with strep throat must stay in bed a few days, must drink a lot of water and fruit juice and soda, and they must take their antibiotic medicine regularly.

Enlarged and infected tonsils sometimes lead to sore throats. Actually, the tonsils can easily get a streptococcus infection, and that will result in the same symptoms as someone with a strep throat. And the treatment is the same, too. Sometimes it takes a few days longer for a child to recover from tonsillitis caused by the streptococcus germ.

Enlarged adenoids, since they are located near the back of the nose, often make a child breathe through the mouth. When you do this constantly, the throat becomes dry and sore. Also, when the throat gets too dry, it begins to hurt and may easily get infected.

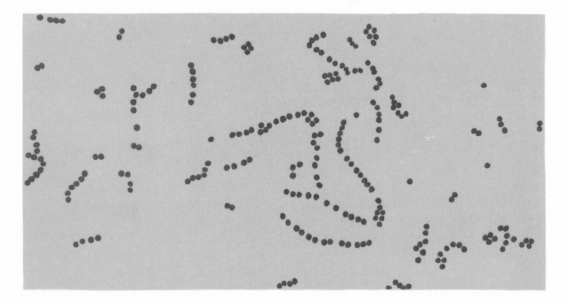

The streptococcus bacterium causes a sore throat that can make a child very ill. Streptococcus grows in long chains, and nowadays the infection it causes can be cleared up quickly with the use of antibiotic medicines.

In China and Japan, children with sore throats or colds wear masks so they won't spread the conditions to others.

This type of sore throat comes back again, time after time, until the adenoids are removed. After that, the child begins to breathe through the nose again, and—no more sore throats from this situation.

Children who live near places where there is a great deal of air pollution, like near a big factory that belches nasty smoke all day, often get sore throats. But now that everybody realizes we must cut down on air pollution, this kind of sore throat shouldn't happen so often.

Don't forget, whenever the outside air is really bad, it is a good idea to close all the windows and stay indoors. And if you happen to have an air-conditioner, turn it on so you can breathe the purer air it produces.

Do you know what they do in some of the Oriental countries when the air is particularly polluted? On those days, a great many people wear surgical masks when they go out in the streets. It helps a little bit to filter out some of the polluting particles, but it is not a terribly efficient way to overcome sore throats from air pollution.

A common cause of sore throats is an allergy. This means that a person is sensitive to a special irritant. For instance, some people get hay fever because they are sensitive to the pollen of certain grasses or trees. Others, and they number millions of children and adults, are allergic to the pollen of the ragweed plant. It means when they

It is a good idea to let our parents know as soon as we feel a scratchy or sore throat.

MY THROAT HURTS!

breathe in the pollen of these grasses or trees or plants, their noses and eyes and mouths become swollen and inflamed. Their noses may get stuffed up and begin to run, their eyes may get red and produce lots of tears, and their throats may get swollen and become sore.

Sore throats due to any kind of allergy can be helped by avoiding the irritating pollen or other substances that are in the air. If they can't be avoided, then the person must take anti-allergic medicines or must take injections to desensitize them from the irritant to which they are sensitive. We'll discuss this more in the chapter on allergies.

If we take good care of ourselves when we have a sore throat, it will clear up quickly. If we don't tell our parents about it and neglect it, we may get into further trouble. Neglected sore throats may lead to further inflammation of the larynx, and we may not be able to talk for a while. Also, if we neglect a sore throat the infection may go down our windpipe and bronchial tubes and into our lungs. Then we'll cough a lot, and get high fever, and may have to spend a couple of weeks in bed. So it is a good idea to let our parents know as soon as we feel a scratchy or sore throat. Prompt treatment will lead to a prompt cure!

Head Injuries

We certainly are lucky that our brains are protected by the nice thick bones of our skull. Think of the many, many times that we bump our head against edges of doors or fall accidentally and strike our poor head on the floor or the ground. Our brains sure would get pretty soft if they didn't have such a strong covering over them.

There aren't many people, children and adults alike, who don't hurt their heads at least once in a while. And it can be painful, can't it? Fortunately, most of these injuries are not serious, and except for a lump and some soreness, we forget about them in a few hours. However, sometimes there can be serious blows and we should never neglect them.

Here is how to tell whether an injury to the head is serious and needs attention by a doctor:

1. Anyone who loses consciousness (faints or passes out) after a head injury should be seen by a doctor. Even if the unconsciousness lasts only a few

Never jump off a high place, even if your playmates dare you to.

seconds, it should be considered serious enough to call the doctor.

The best thing to do for someone who has lost consciousness from being hit on the head is to keep that person absolutely still, even if he or she wants to get up. The person should then be taken to a nearby hospital, preferably by an ambulance.

2. Of course, if someone loses consciousness and stays unconscious after

51

a blow to the head, everyone knows enough to call an ambulance. In almost every community in the country, the police will get an ambulance for an injured person.

3. A person who has an injury to the head and later develops a severe headache should be seen by a doctor.

4. Anyone whose head is injured and who later begins to see things double, or whose sight becomes blurred, should be seen by a doctor.

gets drowsy and falls into a deep sleep must be seen by a doctor, as this may be a sign that there is bleeding inside the skull.

The things we have just described tell us not only that the injury has affected the bones of the skull, but that the brain and blood vessels within the head have also suffered. In many cases, the injury to the brain may be slight and temporary. But our brains are too important to neglect, and it is much

Following a severe head injury, bleeding on the covering of the brain (dura) beneath the skull may lead to the formation of a dangerous blood clot. Bone fragments may be driven into the brain at the site of a blow, causing a brain injury on the opposite side of the skull.

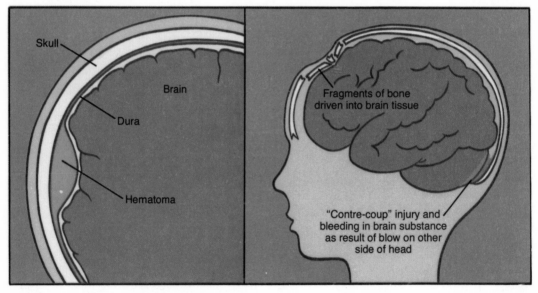

5. If bleeding from the nose or ears takes place after a head injury, the patient should be seen by a doctor, as this sometimes is an indication that one of the bones of the skull has been broken.

6. Someone who seems to recover quickly from a head injury but later

smarter to keep a child who has suffered a head injury in the hospital for a day or two to make sure he or she is all right. Within a day or two, everyone can be positive that no serious damage to the brain has taken place.

When a child with a head injury goes to the hospital, they will take X rays to

Never dive into shallow or unfamiliar water.

see if any of the bones of the skull have been broken. They will also make tests to find out if any damage to the brain resulted from the blow. After they have found out the exact extent and location of the brain injury, they will know how to treat it. Once in a while, brain surgeons will bore a small hole in the skull to relieve the pressure from the bleeding within the skull. This often controls the situation pretty well, and when the wound heals, it leaves practically no scar.

Most children recover completely from head injuries, even from serious ones. This is because the bones of the skull are so good at protecting the soft brain tissue which lies beneath.

As we point out in the next chapter, bleeding from a cut on the head is seldom very serious. There may be an awful lot of bleeding, but it usually stops by itself sooner or later. And when the cut is stitched, the head is as good as new again.

Here are a few things to do in order to avoid serious head injuries:

1. Always wear a helmet when playing football or riding on a motorcycle.

2. Never dive into shallow water, or into strange water where rocks may be near the surface.

3. Never jump off a high place, even if your playmates dare you to.

4. Don't run or make sudden movements in the dark where you might not see a wall or edge of an open door.

5. If you are in the country, be aware of the possibility of rocks falling down a hill.

6. Don't play with children who throw stones.

Cuts, Bruises, and Scrapes

It is very important to clean a scrape thoroughly so it doesn't get infected. We should scrub the area with ordinary soap and warm water for several minutes until it is really clean.

Sooner or later, everybody gets a cut or a bruise or a scrape. Of course, if we are careful, it won't happen as often as it does when we are careless. Most of these injuries seem much worse than they actually are. For example, some cuts look as if there is an awful lot of bleeding, but most of them stop bleeding by themselves within a few minutes. And since we all have a great deal of blood to spare, it doesn't hurt us to lose a little once in a while. Just think of it, someone who gives a blood transfusion to another person gives about two full glasses of blood, and it doesn't do any harm at all!

For some reason that's hard to explain, boys and girls cut their heads quite often, and these cuts usually bleed like the dickens. But here, too, there is no cause to get frightened, because the bleeding soon stops by itself in a short time.

Broken glass, tin cans, and knives are frequent causes of cuts. When we walk barefoot, it is important for us to know that there are no pieces of broken glass hiding in the dirt or sand; when we open a tin can, we ought to be certain we know how to handle the pull ring so we don't cut our fingers or hand; and when we use or play with knives or other sharp things, we must be specially careful.

Friends of ours like Dumbo and the Three Little Pigs and Donald Duck are much luckier than we are when it comes to cuts and bruises and scrapes. They have much thicker skin than we have on the soles of their feet, so they can run around barefoot without worrying about getting cut. Dumbo and the Three Little Pigs also have much thicker skin on their bodies than we do, and Donald is protected by his feathers, so their skins aren't bruised or cut or scraped as easily as ours. And, of course, they open very few cans of soda, and I'll bet they never owned a jack-knife.

Did you know that most bleeding can be stopped simply by pressing the cut area with clean fingers for a few minutes? It might be a good idea for us to tell you the best things to do when someone cuts himself:

1. First of all, don't get too excited about the amount of blood you see.

2. If the cut is dirty, run lukewarm water from a faucet over it for a few minutes. If this doesn't get rid of all the dirt, take a clean handkerchief or a piece of cotton or gauze, wet it, and gently wipe away the dirt.

3. If the bleeding continues, take the clean handkerchief or cotton or gauze, and put it directly on top of the cut and press down on it firmly and steadily for a few minutes. In most cases, this will stop the bleeding. If it stops, then probably all the cut will need is a Band-aid, or a gauze dressing held in place with some adhesive tape.

4. If the cut still bleeds, it is best to go to a doctor's office or to the emergency room of the nearest hospital. In one of

Scrapes form scabs in a day or two, and the scabs fall off a few weeks later when the skin underneath is completely healed. You should never pick at a scab, because that will lengthen the time it takes the scrape to heal.

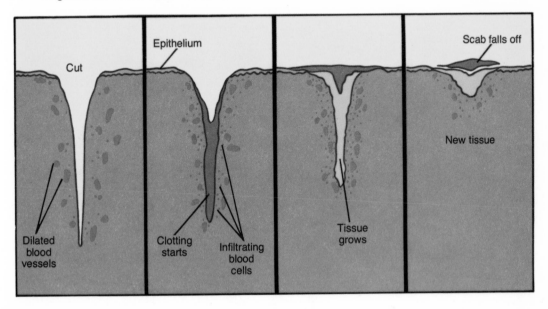

those two places, the doctor will stitch the wound together, and it will be as good as ever within a few days' time.

5. Never pour a strong antiseptic, such as iodine or Mercurochrome, onto an open cut. These medicines may burn the tissues. The best thing to prevent infection in a cut is to wash it thoroughly with water and an ordinary soap.

A word about having a cut stitched: it doesn't really hurt, because when you cut yourself, the edges of the wound become numb and you don't feel pain very well. Also, if the cut is long or deep, the doctor will inject a medicine such as Novocain under the skin edges of the cut to take away the pain. This injection doesn't hurt at all.

Stitches are put in with a needle and thread, almost exactly the way your mother sews a rip in your clothes. Sometimes the stitches are made of black silk, sometimes of nylon, and now there are several new kinds of threads made out of materials that the body can absorb. If this kind of thread is used, the doctor won't have to bother removing the stitches. They will just disappear by themselves.

Stitches are left in anywhere from four to eight or nine days. The longer and deeper the cut, the more days the stitches are kept in place. Of course, as we just mentioned, the stitches that dissolve are left in place indefinitely until they disappear by themselves. But it hurts only slightly to take out

When we walk barefoot, it is important for us to know that there are no pieces of broken glass hiding in the dirt or sand.

stitches, so no one, even little tots, has to be afraid.

Sometimes, when the cut or scrape has been caused by something dirty or rusty, a tetanus shot is given. This doesn't hurt much and will prevent a tetanus infection from taking hold in the injured area.

Bruises come from a hard bump against something, or from being hit hard by a ball or some other solid object that doesn't break open the skin. Bruises mean that the fat and the muscles beneath the skin have been injured and that bleeding has taken place.

Bleeding beneath the skin almost always stops by itself and requires relatively little treatment. Lots of children bump their heads, or fall on their heads, or are hit on the head, and these injuries can lead to a big swelling that hurts a lot for a while. But, of course, anyone can be bruised anywhere on the body.

Here is some advice on what to do if you should be bruised:

1. Wrap some ice in a napkin or handkerchief or towel and press it firmly against the bruised area for ten to fifteen minutes. The ice may stop the bleeding that is taking place beneath the skin.

2. After using the ice for ten to fifteen minutes, replace it with a cold, wet handkerchief or napkin or washcloth or towel for another ten to fifteen minutes.

Bruises may take a few days before the swelling goes down and the discoloration of the skin disappears. If your skin is light in color to begin with, it will be interesting to watch the deep

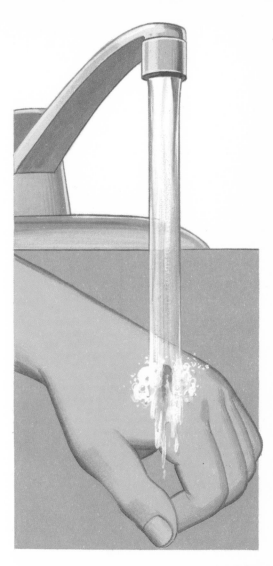

A cut can often be cleaned by running luke-warm water over it, although deep dirt may have to be wiped away.

purple color of the bruise turn lighter over a few days' time. As the bruise heals, the skin turns a bluish-green, then a lighter greenish-yellow, and finally the bruise disappears entirely. And if your skin is brown to begin with, the color of the bruised area will be

When we open a tin can, we ought to be certain we know how to handle the pull ring of the can opener so we don't cut our fingers or hands.

much darker than that of the rest of your skin. But it, too, will lighten and return to normal as the bruise heals.

All children trip and fall and scrape themselves from time to time. It is natural to fall and scrape our skin when we run and play so much, and ride our bikes or skate or ski. And do you know the favorite places to get scrapes? Well, the knees seem to get it very, very often. And sometimes, our elbows or the tip of our noses.

Most scrapes don't bleed very much, but they do ooze a yellowish substance called serum. Serum is made up of blood without the red cells. Scrapes can get infected very easily unless they are treated properly. And when they do get infected, they sometimes leave ugly looking scars when they heal.

Here are things to do when you get a bad scratch or scrape:

1. Since most scrapes happen outdoors, it is not unusual that dirt gets into the wound. As a result, it is very important to clean a scrape thoroughly so it doesn't get infected. To do this, we should scrub the scraped area with ordinary soap and warm water for several minutes until it is clean. And would you believe it? It doesn't really hurt very much to clean a scratch or scrape!

2. After cleaning the scrape, it should be covered with a clean gauze dressing, and the dressing held in place with some adhesive tape. If the scrape hap-

pens to be on the nose or face, we shouldn't cover it at all. It will heal just as well if we leave it exposed to the open air.

3. Scrapes form scabs within a day or two, and the scabs may take a few weeks before they are ready to fall off. They are ready when the skin underneath them has healed completely. It is a very bad idea to pick at a scab. If we do, a new one will form and this will delay the time before it is ready to drop off.

4. If we don't play with the scab and pick at it, and if we don't fall again on the scraped area, most scrapes heal without leaving scars. Some youngsters with scabs on their noses have a habit of picking at them and removing part of the scab before it is ready to come off by itself. Do you know what happens then? A new scab forms! Why, once a boy did this and had a big scab on his nose for almost four months! His friends started calling him "cherry nose," and for a long time after the scab fell off, he had a bright red scar on the tip of his nose.

Luckily, most children have skin that heals quickly and leaves very few bad scars. Even if it looks bad at first, as the child grows older, most scars disappear and are difficult to find even if we look for them. Therefore, never worry too much when you get a severe cut or scrape. It won't damage your good looks. And even if it did, there are surgeons—we call them plastic surgeons—who specialize in getting rid of ugly scars.

A cut or scrape should be thoroughly washed with lukewarm water and soap. Any bleeding usually stops after a few minutes of direct pressure on the cut or scrape. It should then be covered with a gauze bandage, or clean handkerchief.

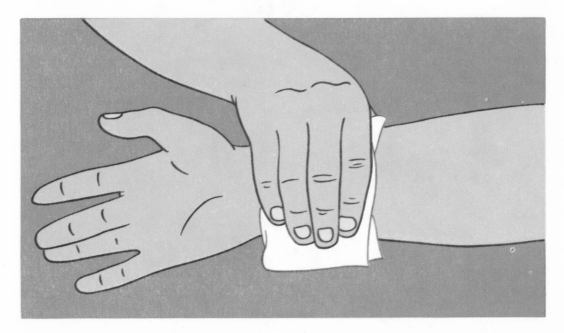

Infections

Youngsters are pretty good at fighting infections, and it doesn't make much difference whether the infection is brought on by bacteria or viruses. But some things are important: Children must be in good general condition, or else it will be much more difficult for them to overcome an infection; furthermore, when they have an infection that affects the whole body, they must make certain to rest in bed and to drink large amounts of fluids.

Everybody is surrounded by various bacteria and viruses all the time. They

We are always surrounded by bacteria and viruses, but our bodies have many built-in defenses that protect us from them.

cover the entire surface of the earth on which we live. They are everywhere—in the air, in the water, on the ground, in the fluids we drink and the food we eat, on the skin of our bodies, in our noses and throats, in our mouths, in the bronchial tubes leading to our lungs, and in our intestines. But most of the sues and the bloodstream of our bodies and we will get sick. For example, unless we take injections against measles, the measles virus can get into our bodies and give us the measles; unless we take injections to protect us against the diphtheria bacteria, we are likely to get this disease.

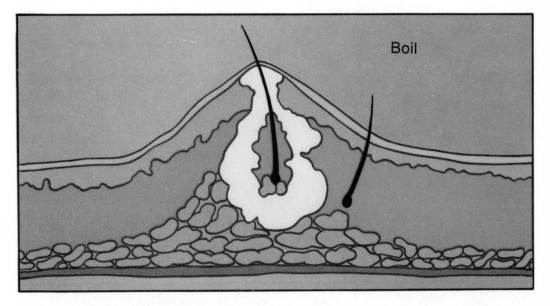

A boil has only one opening, or "head." It is an infection caused by bacteria, most often a staphylococcus germ, and can appear anywhere on the body. A child should not attempt to open a boil himself—this could cause the infection to spread. Boils should be drained by a doctor when the pus is ready to come out.

time, these germs and viruses don't get into our blood or into the tissues of our bodies. They just stay on the surface of our membranes and our skin. As long as they stay on the surface of these structures, they don't cause an infection and they don't make us sick.

Some bacteria and viruses are so powerful that unless we are vaccinated against them, no matter how good our general health, they will enter the tis-

A child's resistance and ability to fight off an infection can be poor if that child is undernourished and lacks the proper amounts of proteins and vitamins. If a child is anemic and has too few red blood cells, it will be more difficult to fight off an infection. And, finally, if a child has a disease in an organ such as the kidneys or the liver or the bone marrow that manufactures white blood cells, the child is more apt to have trouble keeping infections from entering the body and causing illness.

The commonest types of skin infections are called pimples, boils, and abscesses. They can appear anywhere on the body. Pimples are usually no bigger than the size of a pea; a boil may grow to the size of a grape, or a prune, or even larger. Some abscesses are small, while others can grow to the size of a lemon, or even larger.

Pimples, boils, and abscesses are filled with pus, usually cream-colored or a light green color. These infections hurt quite a lot before they are opened by a doctor—or sometimes open by themselves. Then, when the pus comes out, most of the pain disappears within a few hours.

There are certain things that children should remember about pimples, boils, and abscesses:

1. If the infection causes fever, the child should stay in bed. Pimples don't often cause temperature, and many boils don't, either. However, large boils and abscesses do cause fever, and bed rest is important until the temperature returns to normal.

2. Pimples, boils, and abscesses should never be squeezed. This will cause them to spread and grow. Sometimes, if a child squeezes a pimple, it will become a boil. Squeezing a small boil may turn it into a large, spreading abscess.

The commonest types of skin infections are called pimples, boils, and abscesses. They can appear anywhere on the body.

3. The best way to hurry up a pimple, boil, or abscess so that the pus is ready to come out by itself, or ready to be punctured—or lanced—by a doctor, is to apply nice, warm, wet compresses to the area. (A compress is made of a piece of gauze, or a washcloth, or a towel that has been soaked in warm water.) Frequently, a doctor may recommend that the pus will be absorbed by the body instead of draining to the outside.

5. A pimple, boil, or abscess should never be opened until it is "ripe," or until the pus is ready to come out. Many pimples burst by themselves and the pus runs out, but most boils and larger abscesses have to be opened by the doctor. To do this, he gives a little

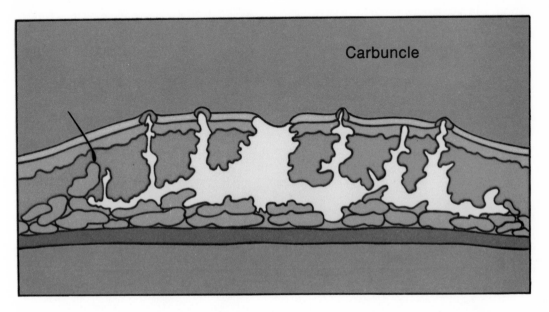

Carbuncle

A carbuncle is a deep-seated infection of the skin, and is different from a boil in that it has more than one "head," or opening. In order to cure a carbuncle, each of the parts of the underlying abscess must be drained. The patient must then rest, drink plenty of liquids, and take antibiotics.

some salt be mixed with the warm water before it is applied to the infected area.

4. Doctors sometimes recommend that children be given an antibiotic medicine to overcome a large boil or abscess. Antibiotics aren't needed for ordinary pimples. But antibiotics may make a boil or abscess disappear, and freezing spray to the area and quickly sticks a knife into the boil or abscess. It is over so quickly that there isn't much pain.

6. Germs that cause pimples, boils, and abscesses can spread to other members of the family, so it is very important to wash your hands thoroughly after touching or treating

such an infection. Also, washcloths, towels, handkerchiefs, and other things that might have pus on them should be boiled so that all the germs are killed.

When someone has a boil or abscess, lymph glands nearby may get enlarged and tender. As we mentioned earlier, the lymph glands help to prevent the germs, or the poisons the germs produce, from getting into the blood and spreading the infection to other parts of the body.

Although viruses can cause many infections that affect the whole body—like measles, German measles, chicken pox, and other childhood diseases—they don't cause pimples, boils, and abscesses. The bacteria that cause most pimples, boils, and abscesses are the staphylococcus germ and the streptococcus germ. Unfortunately, vaccination against these germs doesn't work very well, and as a result we can get infections with these germs over and over again.

Do you know the best way to avoid pimples, boils, abscesses, and other infections? Well, the best way is to keep our resistance high by eating a good diet rich in fresh fruits and vegetables and milk, and by getting plenty of sleep. And one more thing: We should keep our bodies clean so that the germs are washed off our body surface frequently. Children who are always dirty and don't wash their hands often and don't bathe regularly are much more likely to get infections.

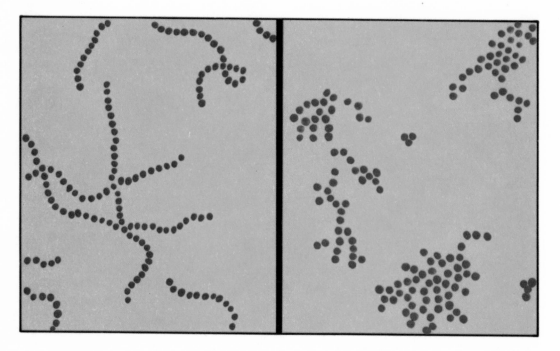

Two germs which may cause infections of the body's various organs are shown in these photomicrographs. Left: the chainlike formation of streptococcus bacteria. Right: the characteristic grapelike clusters of staphylococcus bacteria.

Anemia

Anemia is a condition in which there are too few red cells in the blood or too little iron in the red cells. Sometimes, anemia is caused by too few red cells *and* too little iron in those cells. There are many different kinds of anemia, and before anyone can be cured of the condition, it is necessary to find out what type of anemia is present.

Children frequently do become anemic and, as a result, they may tire easily and have very little pep. Also, anemic children are much more likely to get infections than those who have the right number of red blood cells and the right amount of iron in those red cells.

When we say that the blood has insufficient iron, we really mean that

Some youngsters can look pale and not be anemic at all.

there is too little hemoglobin in the red cells. Hemoglobin gives blood its red color, and it is the hemoglobin within the red cells that carries the oxygen from the lungs to all the tissues of the body. To have a sufficient amount of hemoglobin, we must have a sufficient amount of iron. It is the iron that makes the hemoglobin.

Every cell, every organ, every tissue in the body, requires an adequate supply of oxygen in order to work properly. If there are too few red cells circulating in the arteries, or if the red cells don't contain enough iron, then the organs and tissues won't receive the necessary amount of oxygen.

People used to think that a well-nourished, heavy, or overweight child couldn't be anemic. But we now know that even the huskiest child may be anemic if his diet contains too few vitamins or too little iron or other important minerals. It is simple for a child to stuff himself with candy and cake, or other fattening foods, yet neglect to eat the proper amounts of meats and vegetables and fruits that are so full of vitamins and iron and other necessary minerals. People also used to believe that a child had to look pale in order to be anemic. We now know that lots of children can look healthy and still be anemic. And some youngsters can look pale and not be anemic at all.

Many girls and boys can have a mild anemia without even knowing it. It is only when the anemia continues without treatment that a child begins to lose energy, shows weakness in his muscles, loses his appetite, tires easily, and seems to lose interest in his school-work and playmates. We must remember that the brain needs tremendous amounts of oxygen to function at its best, and if a child has a severe anemia, the brain is just not going to get all the oxygen it needs.

Anemia can be diagnosed simply by pricking the finger with a needle and performing an examination of a little blood under a microscope. Doctors call this examination a blood count. It includes testing to see if there is enough hemoglobin in the red cells and a count to see if there are the right number of red blood cells. Other tests are done, too, in order to distinguish one type of anemia from another. This is important because the treatment will depend upon what type of anemia is present.

Here are some of the various forms of treatment that might be carried out to cure an anemia:

1. If a child is anemic because he has lost a great deal of blood in an accident, a blood transfusion may be given. As we have mentioned elsewhere, the bone marrow manufactures new blood very rapidly. Within a few days, a child may regain all the blood he requires, and it is therefore necessary to give a transfusion only when really large amounts of blood have been lost.

2. If the anemia has resulted from some long-lasting illness, it can be cured only when the long-lasting illness has cleared up. For example, if a child has had a serious kidney infection that has kept him in bed for several weeks, he will probably develop anemia. That anemia will only disappear when the kidney infection is cured.

3. Certain kinds of anemia occur in

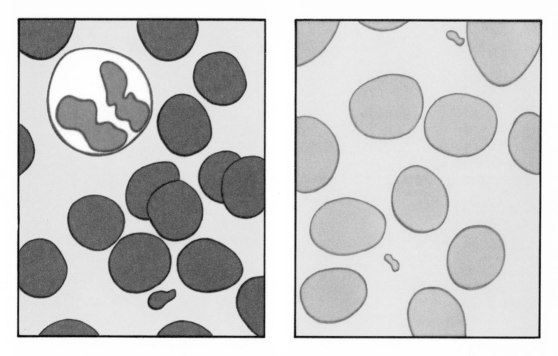

The red blood cells of a person suffering from anemia (right) are a very light pink when stained, and they are often less round and full when viewed under a microscope. The round, plump bodies of normal red blood cells (left), when stained, are a bright pinkish-red. Hemoglobin is the substance that gives normal cells their bright color.

children who suffer from repeated attacks of diarrhea (loose bowel movements). The diarrhea interferes with the absorption of substances that are necessary to form iron and red blood cells. This type of anemia will not clear up until the diarrhea is cured.

4. The commonest type of anemia is due to insufficient iron in the red cells. It is treated by making sure the child eats a proper diet, including plenty of foods rich in iron and other minerals. It can also be treated by giving the child iron pills or, once in a while, by giving injections of iron. Children should remember that liver, meats, green vegetables, and certain fruits contain iron.

5. There are several rather rare kinds of anemia that are present from the time a child is born. For some of these anemias, treatment is difficult. There are certain anemias that require repeated blood transfusions to keep the child healthy; others are often benefited by removing the spleen. One of the spleen's functions is to destroy old red cells, and it has been found that sometimes the spleen destroys healthy red cells as well.

6. Occasionally, a girl will develop anemia when she reaches puberty and starts to change from a child into a woman. Because of this tendency, it is pretty important that older girls make sure to get plenty of iron in their diet when they approach the teen years.

Allergies

We are surrounded by a tremendous number of things in this world. There are millions of plants and trees and flowers; there are millions of insects and fish and furry animals; there are tremendous amounts of dust and pollens that travel through the air on the winds; there are vegetables and fruits and milk and meat and nuts and chocolate candy that we eat; there are cottons and wools and nylons and Dacrons that we use to clothe us or to furnish our homes; there are thousands upon thousands of chemicals that are used to make plastics and deodorants and detergents and cleaning fluids and medicines and other valuable household things; and there are so many other things that we taste and touch and feel every day of our lives that they are too numerous to list.

Nine out of ten children have no trouble with any of the things we have just mentioned. They can breathe anything, eat everything, wear anything, and touch and have close body contact with anything without bad results. But some children are not so lucky! They

An allergic child might be happier living in the middle of a big city where there is a great deal of air pollution but less pollen from weeds and grasses and trees.

68

The bronchial tubes are narrowed due to spasm in an asthmatic attack. To release the spasm and to permit free breathing, it is frequently necessary to give injections of special medications or to breathe in medications through the mouth.

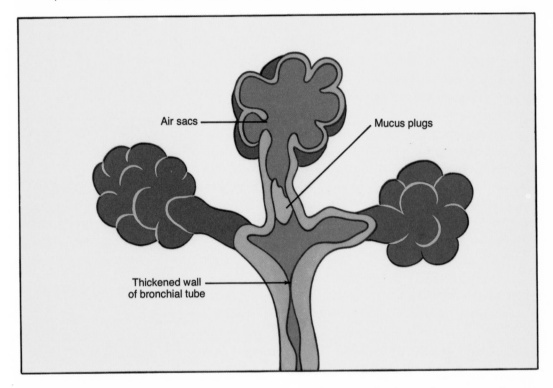

Air sacs

Mucus plugs

Thickened wall
of bronchial tube

may be irritated and made sick by one or more of the things they have breathed, or eaten, or touched. These children are sensitive, or allergic, children. Of course, thank goodness, children are never allergic to everything. Usually, there are just a few things that irritate them and cause them to have an allergic reaction. For example, we knew a child who was allergic only to shrimp, and to absolutely nothing else in the whole world. Or, children may have no food allergies at all, but may be allergic to a pollen or a dust that they breathe. And finally, some children may be able to eat and breathe everything without developing an al-

lergic attack, but they cannot wear nylon or Dacron or wool without breaking out in a skin rash.

There is an old saying, "One man's meat is another man's poison." This is very true insofar as allergies are concerned. A perfectly wonderful thing like cow's milk may make a particular allergic child terribly sick. That same child may be able to drink goat's milk without any bad effect at all!

As we all know, it is healthier to live in the country where there is fresh air to breathe, free from pollution. But, if a child is allergic to the pollen from certain grasses and trees and weeds, he may develop a very serious allergy.

That particular child might be happier living in the middle of a big city where there is a great deal of air pollution but less pollen from weeds and grasses and trees.

We call the things to which a person is sensitive, allergens.

Most doctors agree that the tendency to have allergies is inherited from one's parents or grandparents. There are, however, children who develop an allergy even though their parents and grandparents don't have any. But allergies are much more commonly seen among children whose parents or grandparents *are* allergic.

These are some of the things to which people may be allergic:

Things we breathe

These include pollens, mold spores, animal hairs, dust, smoke, and perfumes.

Pollen is a fine, powdery, yellowish substance produced by grasses and weeds and plants and trees when they are flowering. This pollen is carried through the air from one place to another where it drops onto other grasses and weeds and plants and trees, and causes them to form seeds. The seeds are thus fertilized and can form new grasses and weeds and plants and trees.

Mold spores are much like pollens except that they cause funguses, rather than grasses and plants and trees, to multiply and grow.

In almost any place we live, we breathe in pollens and mold spores and tiny bits of animal hairs and dust and smoke. We can be allergic to none of these things, or one or more of them

A pretty pet is not to be sneezed at, but when baby does it when the cat is close, he may be allergic to animal-hair dander.

eats or drinks, but those most responsible for allergies are: milk, eggs, wheat, fish and seafood, chocolate, nuts, strawberries and other kinds of berries, and spices.

Medicines and drugs

A child can be sensitive to almost any medicine, but perhaps the most frequent allergy is to medicines like aspirin and penicillin. Children may also be sensitive to some vaccines, especially if they happen to be allergic to eggs.

Contact substances

These are things that cause an allergic reaction when we touch or wear them. For example, we may be allergic to poison ivy or other plants, or to rubber, plastics, metals, various dyes, furs, cosmetics, leather, or chemicals.

Infectious substances

Children may be allergic to contact with certain bacteria or viruses or funguses or parasites.

Insect bites

Everyone gets an allergic reaction to the sting of a mosquito or fly or bee or wasp or hornet or scorpion. The itchiness and swelling from the bite of an insect is an allergic reaction.

Physical allergies

These are allergies due to exposure to extreme heat or cold.

The reactions most often seen when someone is allergic depend upon the cause of the allergy. Some of these symptoms are:

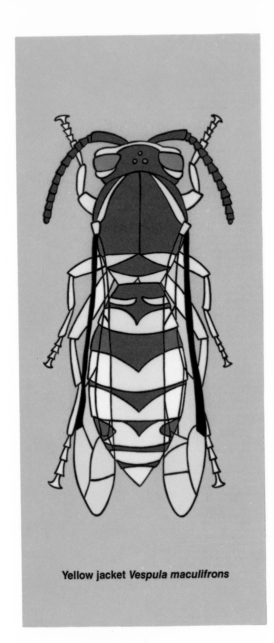

Yellow jacket *Vespula maculifrons*

can cause allergies like hay fever or rose fever or *asthma* or allergic reactions of other kinds.

Foods we eat

Anyone can be allergic to any food he

Children can be allergic to anything they eat, smell, wear, or touch. Very often it is the simplest thing that will cause itching, hives, sneezing, wheezing, or any of the other allergic manifestations. Any child who has an unusual reaction to new or old contacts should be examined for possible allergies.

1. Itching of the skin.
2. Hives, or other skin rashes.
3. Swelling of an eyelid or lip or some other place on the body.
4. Tearing and redness of the eyes.
5. Sneezing.
6. Stuffed up or running nose.
7. Coughing and wheezing.
8. Trouble with breathing.
9. Headache.
10. Nausea and vomiting.
11. Pain in the abdomen and diarrhea.

Parents are pretty bright when it comes to recognizing when their child is having an allergic reaction. Perhaps the first time they may not recognize it, but when the same things happen every time a child eats fish, or every time a child plays with a cat, or every time a child takes an aspirin tablet, the parent comes to understand the situation.

The best way to treat an allergy is to remove the allergen from the child's environment. In other words, if a child is allergic to fish, parents should see to it that the child never eats fish; if a child is allergic to aspirin, he should never be given aspirin; or if a child is allergic to cat fur, he should not own or play with a cat.

Unfortunately, a parent can't always protect a child from every type of allergy. For instance, if a child is allergic to a mold or pollen in the air, the parent can't get that child new air to breathe. Of course, the child *will* feel somewhat better if he or she stays indoors in a house where air-conditioning gets rid of some of the molds and pollens in the air. But children can't *always* stay indoors, can they?

The next best thing to removing the allergen is to take the child to a doctor. who specializes in treating allergic conditions. They are pretty smart in finding out exactly what the child is allergic to, although many tests may have to be given first. They also are pretty successful in treating children with certain medicines and injections to make them less sensitive to the things which give them allergic reactions.

Here are some of the main allergic disorders and what is done for them:

Hay fever

This is a condition in which there is inflammation and redness and itching and tearing of the eyes, a stuffed-up, clogged, or running nose, and itching of the nose and throat. Also, with this, there is an awful lot of sneezing.

Hay fever comes in the springtime and summer when the pollens are flying in the air from grasses and trees.

These pollens often cause hay fever in sensitive children. Pollens are fine, powdery substances produced by flowers and trees and grasses. They are carried through the air to fertilize the seeds of other plants and thus form new ones.

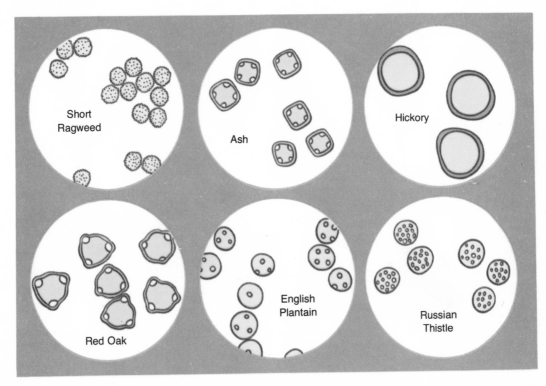

Short Ragweed

Ash

Hickory

Red Oak

English Plantain

Russian Thistle

And hay fever comes in the late summer and fall from the pollens of ragweed and mold spores of funguses. After the child breathes in these pollens or mold spores, his trouble begins.

The treatment for hay fever is to give injections of tiny, tiny amounts of the pollen until a child builds up a resistance to the allergen. By giving the injections, a child can become so much less sensitive to the pollens and mold spores that he gets very few symptoms of hay fever.

If a child does have the inflammation of the eyes, the runny nose, and the other signs of hay fever despite these injections, then the doctor will probably advise that he or she be given antihistamine tablets. These will clear up many of the symptoms and make the child feel much better.

Asthma

Some children don't get hay fever from the usual allergens we have mentioned, but they do get bronchial asthma.

Asthma causes great difficulty in breathing, and during an attack of asthma there is a dry cough, wheezing, and trouble with getting rid of the air breathed in.

In an allergic child, an attack of asthma can be brought on by breathing an unusually large amount of pollen or mold spores. Or, it may be brought on by an infection like a cold or flu, or it can even be brought on by a child being very upset about something.

Asthma is also treated by finding out what allergen is causing the trouble and by giving injections to make the child less sensitive to the irritating substances. Sometimes, in a severe attack of asthma, a child must be taken to the hospital to get special treatment with medicines like adrenalin and cortisone.

Food allergies

To treat food allergies successfully, one must first discover the foods to which the child is allergic. Once this has been done, never let the child eat the food again!

If a child breaks out into hives, or a rash, or has an upset stomach after accidentally having eaten something to which he or she is allergic, antihistamine medications should be given. These medicines may help somewhat, but it may take quite a few days for full recovery from a particular food allergy.

Drug allergies

Medicines and drugs cause the same kind of reactions as food allergies, and are treated in the same way. Of course, every parent knows that it can be dangerous to give a child again a medicine that once produced a bad reaction. A severe attack of a drug allergy may require that the child go to a hospital for treatment with antihistamine medicines, or even treatment with more powerful medicines such as adrenalin and cortisone.

Children who know that they are allergic to certain medicines should carry that information with them wherever they go.

Contact or skin allergies

Skin allergies are caused by contact

of some part of the body with an irritating substance or allergen. Perhaps one of the best known contact allergies is due to touching the poison ivy plant. It can also be caused by hundreds of other substances that come into contact with our bodies.

The first thing to do with contact allergies is to discover exactly what the child is allergic to. Is it certain clothing, or a certain detergent or soap, or a certain plastic? Sometimes, it is not too easy to find a contact allergen; other times it is simple. But once we know, we try to keep that thing away from our bodies.

The rashes of a skin allergy can be very troublesome and may cause a great deal of itching. To relieve it, we apply certain medications. Also, it is frequently advisable to take antihistamine medicines. Once in a while, if the rash continues for a long time even though it has been treated with antihistamines and local medications, it is necessary to give the child a cortisone drug.

Mold spores may cause marked allergic reactions and symptoms similar to those of certain forms of hay fever. Fortunately, the unpleasant symptoms resulting from mold allergies can be greatly relieved by appropriate injections.

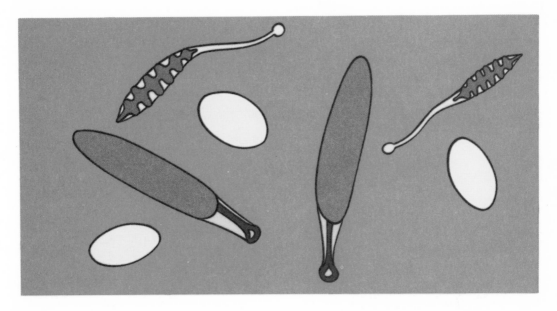

Insect bites and stings

People almost always know what kind of insect bites them. Therefore, they almost always know how to treat the bite. The swelling and itching of an insect bite is best treated by applying a cold compress to reduce the swelling. Also, if the swelling and itching are severe, an antihistamine medicine can be given.

Some children are especially allergic

The cold allergy is treated by giving the patient daily baths with cooler and cooler water until he eventually gets accustomed to the cold. The person with heat allergy is given baths with warmer and warmer water until he eventually gets used to the heat!

A child who gets enough rest is not so likely to show allergic symptoms as a child who is often fatigued.

to the stings of bees and wasps and hornets. If such children are going to camp, or live in an area where there are a great many bees or wasps or hornets, they should be given a series of injections to make them less sensitive to the stings of these insects.

Physical allergy

Children who are especially sensitive to heat or cold may break out in hives, or they may get an attack of asthma, or they may even faint. There are three ways to treat physical allergies:

1. If the patient can move somewhere that isn't too hot or too cold, the allergy will disappear.

2. The acute attack is treated by antihistamine medicines and by taking the person with a heat allergy into a cooler place, or by taking the person with a cold allergy into a warmer place.

3. Some physical allergies can be overcome by making the patient less sensitive to the allergen. For example, the cold allergy is treated by giving the patient daily baths with cooler and cooler water until he eventually gets accustomed to the cold. The person with a heat allergy is given baths with warmer and warmer water until he eventually gets used to the heat.

Allergies sometimes last for a lifetime, but most people learn how to handle their condition so that they don't suffer too much. As children grow older, they learn what brings on allergic attacks and what to do to avoid them or to treat them before they become severe.

Growing Pains

When a muscle has been overworked from hard play and exercise, or has been strained, it may contract very strongly and not be able to relax.

From time to time boys and girls may feel pain in their hips, thighs, or legs. These pains come and go, sometimes during the day and sometimes while in bed at night. People used to think that these pains were caused as the child's muscles and bones were growing. That is why they were called "growing pains." But nobody thinks that anymore. Doctors say that no pain at all comes from the natural growing of muscles or joints or tendons or bones. Instead, they think that these aches and pains result from muscle strain or muscle spasm.

Do you know what a strain is? Well, it is an overstretching of a muscle or tendon due to strenuous exercise. If someone twists his joints very hard, or falls when running fast, he or she might easily strain a muscle or tendon. But the pain from the strain might not come on until several hours later. By that time, the child may have forgotten about straining himself or herself.

Do you know what a muscle spasm is? Well, when a muscle has been overworked from hard play and exercise, or has been strained, it may contract very strongly and not be able to relax. In other words, it tightens and can't loosen itself. This is called a spasm, and if it keeps up for very long, it can be extremely painful. Some people call muscle spasms "muscle cramps."

Growing pains are not so severe that we have to do much about them. Perhaps we should be a little more careful how we play and run, but certainly, we shouldn't stop our play activities just because we get pains once in a while. If the pains are severe, lying in a nice hot tub for twenty minutes to a half hour usually relieves the problem.

Sprains and Broken Bones

The wild way some children play, it is no wonder they sprain a muscle or ligament, twist an ankle or knee, and sometimes even break a bone. The remarkable thing is that sprains and broken bones don't happen more often. Luckily, children have muscles and ligaments and tendons that are much more elastic than they are in grown-ups. Therefore, they can stretch to greater lengths without tearing. Also, a child's knees are much less brittle than grown-ups', so they can stand greater strain without tearing a ligament or cartilage or breaking a bone.

When athletes train to play a strenuous game like football or basketball or baseball or hockey, or when they go skiing, they are taught how to fall so that they avoid serious injury. Did you know that more injuries happen from trying *not* to fall than from falling? It's true. An athlete must learn how to roll with a fall and not to tighten his muscles and ligaments. And often, it's better to lose one's balance rather than to try to keep it. By relaxing his muscles, allowing himself to fall and rolling with the fall, an athlete—and a young person, too—gets hurt less often. Next time you watch a football game, notice how many somersaults the players make when they are tackled or blocked.

Treatment of Fractures

Bone Fractured	Usual treatment	Period of immobilization	Usual Interval until Full Recovery
Shoulder blade (scapula)	Sling	3 weeks	6 weeks
Collarbone (clavicle)	Figure-eight bandage Traction Surgery	3–4 weeks 3–4 weeks 3 weeks	6–8 weeks 6–8 weeks 6–8 weeks
Armbone (humerus) 1. *Neck of humerus*	Sling Velpeau bandage	3–4 weeks 3–4 weeks	8–10 weeks 8–10 weeks
2. *shaft of humerus*	Sling Hanging cast	4–5 weeks 3–5 weeks	8–10 weeks 8–10 weeks
3. *Elbow region*	Sling Surgery Cast	2–4 weeks 3–5 weeks 3–4 weeks	6–8 weeks 8–10 weeks 8–10 weeks
4. *Epiphyseal separation (at the growth line)*	Cast Surgery	3–4 weeks 3–4 weeks	6–8 weeks 8–10 weeks
Forearm bones 1. *Radius* 　a. *head of radius*	Sling Cast	1–3 weeks 3–4 weeks	3–4 weeks 8 weeks
b. *shaft of radius*	Cast Operation	6–8 weeks 6–8 weeks	3–4 weeks 3–4 weeks
c. *distal end (near wrist)*	Cast	4–5 weeks	10–12 weeks
2. *Ulna* 　a. *olecranon (elbow)*	Cast Operation	4–6 weeks 4–6 weeks	10–12 weeks 3–4 months
b. *shaft of ulna*	Cast Operation	6–10 weeks 6–10 weeks	3–4 months 3–5 months
c. *distal end (near wrist)*	Cast	3 weeks	5–6 weeks
3. *Radius and ulna combined*	Cast Surgery	6–8 weeks 6–8 weeks	3 months 3–5 months
4. *Radius and ulna at distal end (wrist)*	Cast	4–5 weeks	10–12 weeks
Wristbones 1. *Scaphoid*	Cast	2–5 months	4–8 months
2. *Other wristbones*	Cast	3 weeks	6 weeks
Hand 1. *Metacarpals*	Cast Surgery	3 weeks 3 weeks	5–7 weeks 6–8 weeks
2. *Phalanges (fingers)*	Cast Surgery	2–3 weeks 2–3 weeks	4–6 weeks 6–8 weeks

Bone Fractured	Usual Treatment	Period of Immobilization	Usual interval until full recovery
Pelvis	Bed rest	4–6 weeks	10 weeks
Thighbone (femur)			
1. *Neck (near hip)*	Surgery	0–3 months	6 months
2. *Intertrochanteric area (near hip)*	Surgery	0–3 months	6 months
3. *Shaft of thighbone*	Cast Traction Surgery	3–4 months 3–4 months 3–4 months	6–8 months 6–8 months 6–8 months
4. *Supracondylar area (near knee)*	Cast	8 weeks	4 months
Kneecap (patella)	Cast Surgery	3–6 weeks 3–6 weeks	4 months 4 months
Leg			
1. *Shinbone (tibia)* a. *condyle (upper end)*	Cast Traction Operation	1–2 months 1–2 months 2–3 months	2–3 months 2–3 months 4–6 months
b. *midshaft*	Cast Surgery	3–6 months 3–6 months	6–8 months 9–12 months
c. *distal end (lower third)*	Cast Surgery	3–6 months 3–6 months	6–8 months 9–12 months
2. *Fibula*	Bandage Cast	2 weeks 3 weeks	3 weeks 5 weeks
Ankle			
1. *Medial malleolus (tibia)*	Cast Surgery	4–8 weeks 6–8 weeks	10–12 weeks 12–14 weeks
2. *Lateral malleolus (fibula)*	Cast Surgery	4–6 weeks 4–6 weeks	6–10 weeks 8–12 weeks
3. *Bi- or tri-malleolar (tibia and fibula)*	Cast Surgery	6–12 weeks 6–12 weeks	4–6 months 4–8 months
Foot			
1. *Tarsals* a. *os calcis (heelbone)*	Cast Surgery	1–3 months 2–3 months	2–6 months 3–6 months
b. *others (footbones)*	Cast Surgery	6–10 weeks 6–10 weeks	4–6 months 4–6 months
2. *Metatarsals*	Cast	3–6 weeks	6–8 weeks
3. *Phalanges (toes)*	Cast	2–6 weeks	3–8 weeks
Ribs	Strapping Injection	1–3 weeks 0–3 weeks	3–6 weeks 3–6 weeks

Girls play almost as many strenuous games as boys, and so they, too, strain muscles and ligaments, and break a bone occasionally. And when a girl skis or plays hockey or basketball or tennis, she must do the same things the boys do if she wants to avoid serious injury.

People used to be happy when their doctors told them that a bone was not broken and that the injury was only a strain or a torn ligament or cartilage. Now we realize that some sprains and tears of ligaments or cartilages are just as serious, and sometimes more serious, than a broken bone. Injuries to the ligaments and cartilages of the knee are extremely common in girls as well as in boys, and they often cause more trouble and take longer to heal than a fractured bone. (The word fractured means broken). In some cases all a broken bone needs is a plaster cast for a few weeks, but some tears of ligaments or cartilages may need an operation to repair them.

Muscle sprains and sprained or torn ligaments or cartilages are very painful when they happen. The best first-aid treatment for such an injury is to keep the arm or the leg as still as possible and not to move it. Certainly no one should try to walk on an injured hip, knee, or ankle. If he does, he may make the injury a lot worse. A good deal of bleeding beneath the skin usually takes place when a muscle or ligament is torn. As a result, there will be a great deal of swelling in the area. Soon after the tear one may sometimes notice that the skin around the area is taking on a bluish color. This is caused by bleeding that has taken place under the skin.

The only sure way to know whether a bone is broken is to take an X ray, and this, as we know, must be done either in a doctor's office or in a hospital. If a bone is found to be broken, the doctor will see whether the broken parts are separated and out of line. If the broken parts are out of place, the doctor "sets" or "reduces" the fracture. This means that he puts the broken parts back into their normal position. To set a fracture, the patient is usually given an anesthetic so he can go to sleep and feel no pain while the bones are being handled and put back in place. Occasionally, it is possible to set a fracture just by giving an injection of a local anesthetic, like Novocain, into the area of the break. In these cases, the patient feels no pain, either, but does not go to sleep.

After putting the broken bones back into their proper position, the doctor must make sure that they stay that way until they are completely healed. He does this usually by putting on a plaster cast. A cast is a bandage that is wet when first put on but later dries out and becomes hard and stiff. The stiffness and hardness of the cast protects the broken bones and keeps them from moving out of position. Once in a while, when the bones are broken in several places or are far out of position, the doctor will have to operate to put them together again. When he has done that, he sometimes keeps them in place by wrapping a wire around them or by putting in a metal plate from one part of the broken bone to the other. Naturally, these operations are done under anesthesia while the patient is asleep.

If the X rays show that a bone is

The only sure way to know whether a bone is broken is to take an X-ray, and this, as we know, must be done either in a doctor's office or in a hospital.

broken but the broken parts are not out of place, then a cast is applied while the patient is awake. It is not painful to put on a cast. Also, it doesn't hurt when a cast is removed, although the electric machine they use to cut a cast makes an awful racket.

A cast should be put on so that it prevents movement of the broken bones. To do this, the cast must cover the joints both above and below the break. As an example, if someone breaks a leg, the cast must cover the foot, ankle, and the knee. If someone breaks an arm, the cast may have to go from the hand all the way up to the shoulder.

Casts stay on anywhere from three weeks to three or more months, depending upon which bones are broken and how badly they are broken. Naturally, if the broken bones are not out of

83

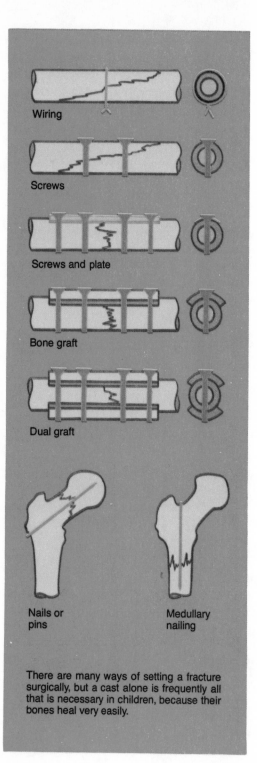

Wiring

Screws

Screws and plate

Bone graft

Dual graft

Nails or pins

Medullary nailing

There are many ways of setting a fracture surgically, but a cast alone is frequently all that is necessary in children, because their bones heal very easily.

place, a cast will not have to stay on nearly as long as when the bones are badly broken and are far out of their normal position.

Plaster casts are sometimes used for arms and legs when there is a severe muscle or ligament tear, even if no bone is broken. As mentioned before, some muscle and ligament injuries cause just as much trouble and take just as long to heal as some fractures. Casts are also applied in certain cases where the back has been badly injured. In these cases, the cast is applied to the entire body from the chest down to the hips.

There are certain rules everybody with a cast should follow:

1. Don't allow a cast to get wet in a bath or shower. It won't make much difference if it gets wet in the rain, as it will dry out quickly. Also, if we accidentally spill something on it, no great damage will be done.

2. No one should walk or put full weight on a cast unless the doctor has given permission to do so. Some casts can have special walking attachments put on, and then, it is O.K. to walk on them. People should know that walking or placing weight on a cast without the doctor's permission may cause the cast to crack or break. Then, the fractured bone may get out of position. And even if that does not happen, it may become necessary to put on a new cast to replace the damaged one.

3. Don't try to trim the edges of a cast by yourself. If necessary, the doctor will do it.

4. If there is a lot of itching beneath the cast, ask your doctor what to do about it. Don't go poking things be-

neath your cast; you may scratch your skin or get a skin infection, and they might have to remove the cast before it is ready to come off.

5. It is perfectly O.K. to have your friends write or draw pictures on your cast. That won't hurt it.

A sprained or torn muscle, ligament, or tendon may be painful for several days, or even weeks. Most broken bones, however, stop hurting within a couple of days after a cast has been put on. The reason a bad sprain or tear of a ligament or muscle hurts longer than a fracture is that there are many sensitive nerves in muscles and ligaments, but bones do not have so many nerves.

Did you know that people have more than two hundred bones in their bodies, and that the chances are very great that they will some day break one of them? But we shouldn't worry too much when we do break a bone because when it heals, it is as strong as ever! And even if the arm or leg looks funny when the cast comes off, it will look normal again in a few weeks' or months' time. Children, especially, should not worry if an arm or leg looks a little crooked after recovering from a fracture. Childrens' bones straighten out as the child grows older, even if they looked strange right after the cast came off.

It is perfectly okay to have your friends write or draw pictures on your cast. That won't hurt it.

Catching Cold

Stay as far away as you can from someone who is sneezing or coughing because he has a cold.

Everyone hates to get a cold. Who wants to have his nose run or to cough or to feel stuffed up, anyway? And then, too, most colds are accompanied by a sore throat, a fever, and eyes that are red and teary. Sometimes, when a child has a cold, he develops aches and pains in his muscles in various places in the body. And, of course, we know that a bad cold means not going to school, no playing outdoors, no movies, no going to parties. Most times, a bad cold means lying around the house or being in bed for a few days. That's not much fun. And, finally, what fun is it to take medicines even if they do get you to feel better?

Do you want to know something? Mickey Mouse and Donald Duck and Pluto practically never get colds. It is strange but they seem to know better how to take care of themselves than we do. And even if our animal friends did catch cold, we wouldn't catch it from them because their germs and viruses don't often infect human beings. And our germs and viruses that cause colds don't seem to affect them, either. But you just sneeze without covering your nose, or cough without covering your mouth, and you can give a cold to anyone who is in the same room with you.

Every once in a while, no matter how careful we are, we do get a cold. But if we follow certain good rules, we won't get colds very often. Here's what all of us, grown-ups as well as children, should do:

1. Don't kiss or hug anyone, big or small, who has a cold. Colds are so contagious that one hug or kiss may cause you to catch it.

2. Stay as far away as you can from someone who is sneezing or coughing because he has a cold. Actually, people who have colds should stay in their own rooms as much as possible. (Incidentally, I wonder how often Sneezy gave colds to Sleepy, Dopey, Happy, Bashful, and Grumpy? I'll bet he didn't give them very often to Doc. Doc was too smart—he knew enough to keep his distance whenever Sneezy let go with one of his big blasts.)

3. If you can help it, never walk around with wet or damp feet. Put on your rubbers or boots before going out in the rain or snow. And if you accidentally get caught in the rain or snow without your rubbers or boots, head for home where you can dry out. Remember, you can miss a lot of fun and good times by catching a cold unnecessarily.

4. Another thing that seems to bring on a cold is getting chilled, especially after being overheated from playing. Don't forget that clothing gets damp and wet from perspiration. And many children, instead of going home to change into dry clothing, hang around in wet clothes and get chilled. Cooling off too quickly after being overheated, especially in cold weather, may lead to a cold.

5. Getting part of the body in a cold draft seems to bring on colds in some people. It is odd, but exposing the entire body to wind and cold, as we often do on wintry days when we go outdoors, does not seem to cause a cold nearly as often as when only part of our body is exposed to cold or wind.

6. Of course, a child who doesn't dress warmly enough when he goes out in chilly or cold weather takes a great chance of getting a cold. Mothers and fathers are pretty smart when it comes to knowing what their children should wear, and it is a good idea to take their advice when they tell you how to dress.

A good way to avoid catching cold is to never walk around with wet or damp feet and clothing. Always wear proper clothes when you have to go out in the rain or snow. And if you do get caught out in the rain without protection, head for home, where you can dry out.

All too often, when youngsters refuse to put on a sweater or coat in cold weather, they punish themselves by getting colds.

7. Many doctors believe that people catch more colds when they neglect to eat the right foods. For example, we should always eat plenty of fresh fruits and vegetables. This will supply us with most of the vitamins we need. Those who have a vitamin deficiency seem to catch colds very frequently.

If we are unlucky enough to catch a cold, we certainly don't want to give it to other members of our family, or to our playmates. Here are some good ways not to spread colds:

1. Always cover your mouth with your hand when coughing. This will help to stop the spread of the cold viruses.

2. When sneezing, always sneeze into a tissue or handkerchief. A tissue is better than a handkerchief because it can be thrown away.

3. If a sneeze comes on very suddenly and there is no time to get a tissue or handkerchief, sneeze into your hands and cover your nose.

4. Don't kiss or hug anyone until your cold is all better.

5. Don't play in the same room with anyone while you are still sneezing or coughing from a cold. Your mom or dad will know when you have recovered sufficiently to play with others.

6. Go to parties or play groups or to school only after your cold is better. This may take as long as four or five days if it is a bad cold.

Don't play in the same room with anyone while you are still sneezing or coughing from a cold.

Sinus Infections

The ordinary cold, followed by an infection of a sinus, is seen in large numbers of children who live in places where the temperature changes greatly from season to season. Children who live in climates where it is nice and sunny and warm most of the time do occasionally get sinus infections, but not nearly so often as those who live where it rains and snows and is damp and cold a lot. To a certain extent, all children can protect themselves against sinus infections and other illnesses affecting the nose and throat, but those who live in wet, cold places can't protect themselves as well as those who live where the weather is always nice.

The sinuses are empty spaces—called cavities—in the bones surrounding the nose. Their purpose is to make the bones of the skull lighter and to make the voice sound better when we speak. When the sinuses are infected, our

89

voices often sound as if we had a clothespin clamped across our nostrils. Just pinch your nostrils shut and then speak; you'll see how your voice would sound if you had a sinus infection.

There are eight sinuses in the head, and each one of them has an opening that connects with the inside of the nose. Each sinus is lined with a mem-

teria (germs). If the cold is taken good care of, in all probability the infection will not spread into the sinuses. But if the patient is careless and gets overheated or overtired, or dives and swims a lot under water, the membranes of the sinuses may get inflamed, too. And although most colds are caused by viruses, in neglected cases germs such

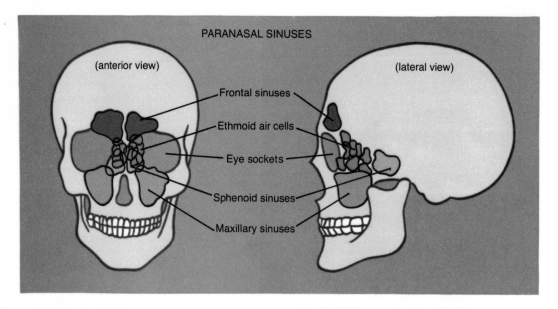

PARANASAL SINUSES

(anterior view)

(lateral view)

Frontal sinuses

Ethmoid air cells

Eye sockets

Sphenoid sinuses

Maxillary sinuses

There are 4 pairs of nasal sinuses, as shown in the diagram above. These sinuses are air spaces within the skull. Their main purpose is to lighten the weight of the skull and to give resonance to the voice. They are also a frequent site of infection.

brane, much like the membrane that lines the inside of the nose. These membranes normally secrete a little watery mucus that keeps the sinuses and the inside of the nose from becoming too dry.

When someone has a cold, the membranes of the nose become inflamed and swollen. Most such colds are caused by viruses rather than by bac-

as streptococci and staphylococci may take hold and cause an infection within the nearby sinuses.

A child can get a sinus infection without first having a cold. One of the commonest ways to get a sinus infection is to dive and swim underwater in a pool or lake where the water is not too clean. Then the contaminated water gets into the sinuses and creates an infection. Also, youngsters with allergies such as hay fever seem to get sinus infections more often than those who have no allergies.

Here are the ways we know there is trouble in one or more of our sinuses:

1. A cold may last much longer than usual and the nose stays stuffed for two or more weeks after the start of the cold.

2. A child may develop headaches with his cold. These headaches are worse when the head is down and the child bends over.

3. The voice sounds flat and nasal.

4. Mucus keeps draining out of the nose and down the back of the throat. This often causes a great deal of coughing, especially when the child is lying down.

5. There is pain when pressing over the sinuses at the sides of the nose or on the bones over the eyes.

6. If the infection is severe, the patient will have fever and will feel generally sick.

7. In many cases, X rays of the sinuses will show that they are infected.

Here are some things the doctor may prescribe in order to cure a sinus infection:

1. Rest in bed for a few days until the temperature is normal and the child feels better.

2. Apply warm compresses to the face, using a washcloth or towel. This may relieve some of the pain and might help to drain out some of the pus that

Special nasal sprays or nose drops are given to shrink the inflammation of the membranes and thus allow the mucus to drain better.

One of the commonest ways to get a sinus infection is to dive and swim underwater in a pool or lake where the water is not too clean. When contaminated water is driven up into the sinuses, it can create a sinus infection.

has collected in the sinuses.

3. Breathing in steam, either from a faucet, a steam kettle, or a steam inhaler, often helps to get the mucus and pus to drain out of the sinuses more easily.

4. Special nasal sprays or nose drops are sometimes given to shrink the inflammation of the membranes and thus allow the mucus and pus to drain better.

5. Antibiotic medicines are given to kill the germs that have gotten into the sinuses.

Most sinus infections will clear up within a couple of weeks, but there is a tendency for them to come back again if people aren't specially careful when they get their next cold. To prevent this from happening, when the next cold rolls around, here are some things

to do:

1. The cold should be treated by rest in bed until everyone is absolutely sure that there is no temperature for at least two days.

2. If there is any fever, antibiotic medicines might be given. This will not cure the cold, but it may prevent a sinus infection from developing.

3. Drafts and cold air should be avoided.

4. No one should ever blow his nose too hard, even if it means that some of the mucus stays up in the nose. Hard nose-blowing may force some of the infected mucus to go from the nose into the sinuses.

5. If the child has allergies, these should be treated by a specialist who knows how to control them, thus lessening the chances of a sinus infection.

Bronchitis

Bronchitis is an inflammation of the air passages leading to the lungs. Actually, the condition should be called tracheobronchitis because the trachea (the windpipe in the neck and upper chest) is almost always involved in the inflammation, too.

Bronchitis often comes on after a very bad cold or sinus infection. It is usually caused by a virus. Germs such as the streptococcus and the pneumonia germ can also cause bronchitis.

Most children who take good care of themselves when they have a cold don't get bronchitis. However, if a child is anemic, or too thin, or neglects to stay in bed and do what he is told when he has a cold, he is more likely to develop bronchitis. Also, youngsters with allergies seem to get bronchitis more often. Wintry, damp weather also makes it easier for the viruses and germs to infect the bronchial tubes.

Here is how a doctor knows that a child has bronchitis:

1. There is a great deal of coughing, often bringing up large amounts of mucus or pus.

2. The temperature goes up, sometimes as high as 102° to 103°.

3. On listening to the chest with a stethoscope, the doctor will hear squeaky sounds called *rhonchi*.

It is important to take special care of a boy or girl who has bronchitis because, if not treated properly, pneumonia (an infection of the lungs) may develop.

This is the way most cases of bronchitis are treated:

1. The child should stay in bed until his temperature has been normal for at least two days.

On listening to the chest with a stethoscope, the doctor will hear squeaky sounds called rhonchi.

2. A good deal of the time in bed should be spent in a sitting or semisitting position. This makes it easier to cough up mucus and pus from the bronchial tubes.

3. The air in the bedroom should be kept warm and moist. Dry, cold air tends to irritate the bronchial tubes.

4. Cough medicines are given to help the child bring up and get rid of the mucus or pus.

5. Aspirin, or some other drug with the same effect as aspirin, is given to relieve aching pains and to bring the temperature down to normal.

6. Antibiotic medicines are frequently given if the fever isn't controlled by giving aspirin, or if the bronchitis lasts longer than a few days. By giving antibotics,, the child is often protected against developing pneumonia.

Children with severe cases of bronchitis may take a couple of weeks, or even more, to fully recover. And if we want to do our best to prevent another attack of bronchitis, here are some things that should be investigated:

1. If a child has a sinus infection, it should be treated. Sinus infections quite often lead to bronchitis.

2. Infected tonsils and adenoids should be removed because they may lead to an attack of bronchitis.

3. Allergies should be controlled as best as possible. As mentioned before, allergic children are more apt to get attacks of bronchitis.

4. If a child is underweight or anemic or doesn't have enough vitamins in his diet, these situations should be corrected. Lowered resistance results from being anemic and underweight, thus making it much easier for viruses or germs to invade the bronchial tubes.

Bronchitis is an inflammation of the air passages leading to the lungs. It causes fluid to collect in the bronchial tubes and air cells, and if not treated, may result in pneumonia.

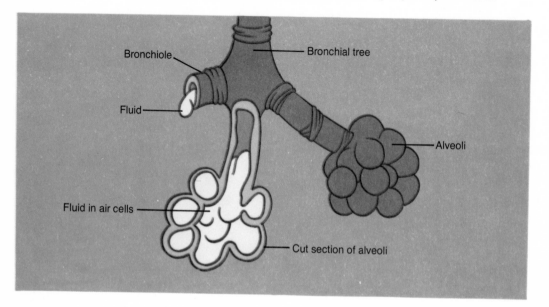

Influenza

Large amounts of water, fruit juices, and other liquids should be taken. This will help to flush the poison from the influenza virus out of the body and will aid in getting rid of the fever.

Influenza is a disease caused by a virus. It affects the nose, throat, windpipe, bronchial tubes, and lungs. Of all the contagious diseases, influenza is one of the most easily spread from one person to another. There are many different kinds of influenza viruses; some cause only a mild illness, others can make a person extremely sick. A popular name for influenza is the flu. Mild cases used to be called grippe, but that name is not used much anymore.

Influenza is so contagious and the virus is so widely present that huge numbers of people can be affected at a time. In some epidemics, millions of people in one part of the country may get the disease within just a few weeks' time. The two main viruses of influenza are called Influenza virus A and Influenza virus B.

Scientists who study contagious diseases are able to tell when and where epidemics of influenza can be expected to break out. For example, if there is an epidemic of influenza in Europe or Asia, these scientists can usually guess when the disease will strike the United

95

States, and what part of the country will be hit hardest. They can also forecast fairly accurately how many people will catch the disease. In some epidemics, one out of every three or four children can be expected to get the disease. Luckily, in most cases, the condition is mild, especially if one has been vaccinated beforehand.

Epidemics of influenza don't come

Here are some of the symptoms of influenza:

1. Fever. In some cases it may go as high as 104°.

2. Marked aches and pains in the muscles and joints throughout the body, especially in the back and thighs and legs.

3. A runny nose, with discharge of mucus from the throat and bronchial

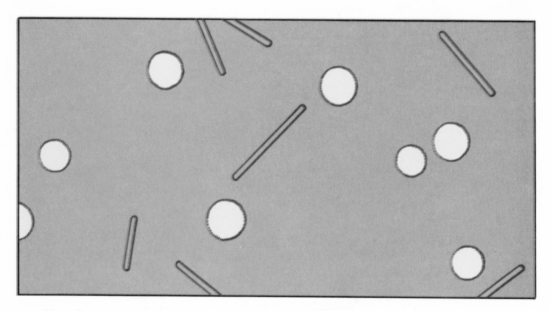

Magnified by an electron microscope, Asian influenza virus particles can be seen as round dots. The long lines are bacteria. These germs can be seen only with the aid of a powerful microscope that magnifies them tens of thousands of times.

every year. For some peculiar reason, the virus doesn't attack many people one year but may hit extremely hard another year. But to be safe, people should do their best to prevent the disease each year by getting influenza vaccine injections. Since the condition comes most often in the winter and early spring, it is wise to get your flu shot late in the fall.

tubes as well.

4. Cough, with the bringing up of yellow or greenish muscus.

5. Weakness and tiredness with lack of pep and energy and a strong desire just to lie in bed and do nothing, not even to look at television.

6. Headache, and sometimes a sick-to-the-stomach feeling.

7. When the doctor has a blood count

taken, it is usually found that there are fewer than the normal number of white blood cells.

The severe symptoms of influenza last for five to six days, but it takes another couple of weeks before the patient begins to feel normal again. During the time he or she is sick, the influenza patient must be kept away from friends and family members, because influenza is so terribly contagious. The disease is spread by coughing or sneezing. It is therefore important to teach everyone with the flu, and also those who just have a simple cold, to cover his mouth when he coughs and to cover his nose when he sneezes!

Most youngsters recover from influenza without complications, but here are things to do to make sure everything goes well:

1. Stay in bed until temperature has been normal for three days.

2. Aspirin, or a similar medicine, should be taken to relieve the aches and pains, and to help bring down the temperature to normal.

3. Large amounts of water, fruit juices, and other liquids should be taken. This will help to flush the poison from the influenza virus out of the body and will aid in getting rid of the fever.

Many doctors think it is wise to keep children who are allergic to flu vaccine home from school during an influenza epidemic.

4. Room temperature should be comfortably warm and the air in the bedroom should be moist. This will help the patient to bring up the mucus when he coughs.

5. If coughing is severe, a cough medicine is given.

6. In order to prevent complications like an ear infection or pneumonia, antibiotic medicines are given. Unfortunately, the antibiotics aren't very effective in killing the influenza virus.

Of course, it is much smarter to prevent influenza than it is to cure it once it has infected a child. To do this, doctors recommend that children be given influenza vaccine. The vaccine should be given a month or two before the epidemic is expected to strike. It would be nice if the vaccine always worked, but it is thought that it protects against influenza in only about seven out of ten people who take the shots. But the three who get influenza anyway, even though they received the vaccine, will probably get mild cases.

Children who are allergic to eggs cannot be given flu vaccine, because the vaccine is manufactured by growing it in chicken eggs. Therefore, if they were given the vaccine, they would get an allergic reaction. Many doctors think it is wise to keep children who have not received the vaccine, because of their allergy, home from school during an influenza epidemic.

Influenza vaccine has proved to be effective in protecting children from the disease. To prepare vaccine, viruses are injected into chicken eggs that are placed in incubators to promote viral growth. Eventually, the virus is removed from the eggs and processed to yield vaccine.

Pneumonia

HACK!
HOCK!
COFF!

Pneumonia is an infection of the lungs, caused either by a bacteria or a virus. The commonest bacteria is a germ called the pneumococcus, but the disease can also be caused by other bacteria such as the streptococcus, the staphylococcus, Klebsiella, and others. One of the most common viruses to affect the lungs is the influenza virus.

Pneumonia used to be much more common and serious than it is now. Today, people don't get pneumonia as often because they take better care of themselves when they have a cold or sore throat or grippe or bronchitis or influenza. Also, the antibiotic medications kill many of the germs that cause pneumonia, and if a patient is given antibiotics when he has bronchitis or influenza, or some other infection of the nose or air passages, he is less likely to develop a lung infection such as pneumonia.

Some types of pneumonia come on

suddenly with a high fever, a chill, a cough, and a pain in the chest. In many cases, the patient has had a cold or other infection for a few days before the symptoms of the pneumonia begin. Within a few hours after the onset of pneumonia, the patient begins to breathe more rapidly and may feel short of breath. Next, he may begin to cough up mucus that is pink-colored or contains little streaks of blood. Usually, someone with pneumonia loses his appetite and may vomit if he attempts to eat too much.

When a doctor examines the chest of a patient with pneumonia, he will hear abnormal sounds through his stethoscope. And, if he X-rays the patient's lungs, he will see an abnormal shadow

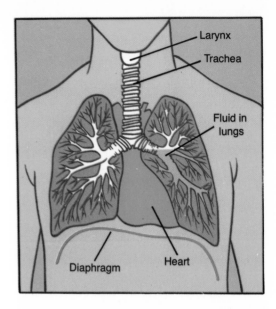

One effect of pneumonia is that the lungs become congested with fluid, which the doctor can detect by listening to a child's chest with a stethoscope. Most cases of pneumonia can be cured by the giving of antibiotic medications.

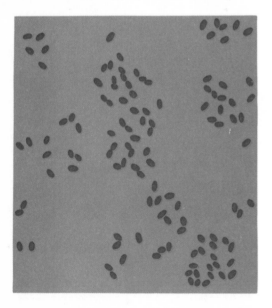

Many different kinds of bacteria, and viruses too, can cause pneumonia. The bacteria shown in this picture are called pneumococci, and they produce a very common type of pneumonia. This type of pneumonia can be cured with antibiotic medications.

in the infected part of the lung where the pneumonia is located. And, finally, when a blood count is taken, it will show an abnormally high white blood cell count.

Here are some of the things that are done in treating pneumonia:

1. Rest in bed. Often, the patient is more comfortable sitting up, rather than lying down flat.

2. Large amounts of fluids are taken, including water, fruit juices, and even soda.

3. Antibiotic medicines are given. The particular antibiotic that is given will depend upon which germ is causing the pneumonia and how sensitive the germ is to the particular antibiotic drug. Although pneumonias caused by

a virus are not cured by giving antibiotics, the antibiotics are given anyway. This is done so that bacteria (which can be killed by the antibiotics) do not attack the lungs that have already been weakened by the virus infection.

4. Oxygen is sometimes given if the patient is very short of breath.

5. If coughing is severe and is interfering with rest and sleep, a cough medicine is given.

6. If the patient is constipated, as frequently happens in cases of pneumonia, a laxative or an enema is given.

Children usually get over a pneumonia caused by bacteria within a week or two. Pneumonia caused by a virus may take several weeks before it completely clears up. However, no matter what kind of pneumonia the patient has had, it will usually take several weeks or even a couple of months before all his or her strength and pep are regained. Children are sometimes anemic after pneumonia, and they may require iron and vitamin pills to help them to feel as strong and energetic as they did before the attack of pneumonia. And, of course, during the period of recovery, children should take it easy and not do strenuous exercise. Also, they should be sure to get plenty of sleep each night.

When a doctor examines the chest of a patient with pneumonia, he will hear abnormal sounds through his stethoscope.

Rheumatic Fever

When rheumatic fever affects the nerves, the condition is known as Saint Vitus' dance because the child's motions make him look as if he were doing some sort of peculiar dance.

Many years ago, rheumatic fever was one of the most common and one of the most serious diseases affecting children. A child with this condition would run a very high fever that would come and go almost every day for a period of a few weeks to a few months. In addition, there would be painful swelling with redness and tenderness of the joints, such as a knee or an ankle or an elbow or a shoulder. Sometimes the pain in the joints would be so severe that the child could not move an arm or stand on a leg. And other organs, too, like the heart, the lungs, and the kidneys, and the nerves, would be affected by the germs that caused rheumatic fever. When the rheumatic fever germs attacked the heart, the heart muscles were frequently damaged and a heart murmur would result. When the nerves were affected, the child often developed jerky, uncontrolled movements of his arms and legs and other muscles of the body that had affected nerves going to them. When rheumatic fever hit the nerves, the condition was known as Saint Vitus' dance, because the child might look as if he were doing some sort of peculiar dance.

Rheumatic fever is caused by a particular type of streptococcus germ. Nowadays, we have extremely powerful antibiotic medicines that can kill these germs. As a result, we don't see many children who develop rheumatic fever after a streptococcus infection. In the days before the wonderful antibiotic drugs were discovered, a child might have an attack of tonsillitis or strep throat, or would have scarlet fever, and a few weeks later, he would develop rheumatic fever. Today, a child with tonsillitis or scarlet fever or strep throat is given antibiotic medications. The germs that would have caused the rheumatic fever are killed by these medications before they can do any serious harm, and the child never gets rheumatic fever.

If a child is unlucky enough to get rheumatic fever, he must stay quietly in bed for several weeks. During that time, he will be given large doses of antibiotics to kill the streptococcus germ. He may also be given large doses of aspirin or some similar medicine to get rid of the pain and swelling in his joints. In some cases, a medicine known as cortisone is also given to control the rheumatic fever.

If a child is obedient and stays quietly in bed and takes his various medicines without too much fuss, the chances are good that no damage will occur to his heart or lungs, or to his nerves or muscles or joints.

It is thought that some cases of rheumatic fever are influenced by infected tonsils that contain a streptococcus germ. Therefore, when a child has fully recovered from an attack of rheumatic fever, the tonsils are removed. But that is not enough to prevent another attack of the disease, because the streptococcus germ may be growing in other places in the body. To prevent another attack of rheumatic fever, children are often given antibiotic medicines every day for months, or even years, at a time.

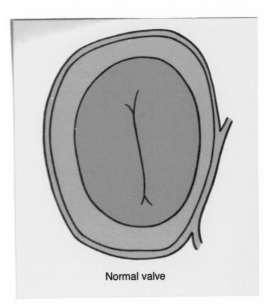

Normal valve

The mitral valve lies between the atrium and ventricles on the left side of the heart. The normal mitral valve is strong and tightly closed.

The mitral valve shown here has been weakened and damaged by disease. Its muscles cannot relax or contract completely. As a result, it has become a leaky valve that won't function normally.

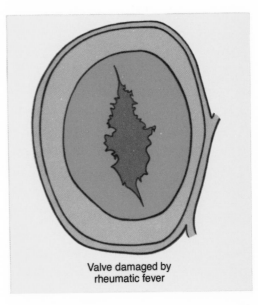

Valve damaged by rheumatic fever

One of the most frequent causes of a pain in the belly is eating too fast and not chewing thoroughly.

Stomachaches

Many people think that the stomach takes up, or occupies, the whole belly area. This is not true, as one can see from the diagram. The stomach is mostly in one corner of the belly, high up on the left side underneath the ribs. In addition to the stomach, the belly, or abdomen, contains the small and the large intestines, the liver, the spleen, the pancreas, the kidneys, and several other organs. And so, when somebody says he has a "stomachache," it might not come from the stomach at all, but from one of the other organs.

Actually, more stomachaches come from the intestines than from the stomach itself. However, in this part of the book we will talk mainly about the various causes of pain in the belly, whether that pain comes from some disorder in the stomach or some other organ.

Here are some common causes of pain in the belly and what should be done about them:

Upset Stomach

One of the most frequent causes of a pain in the belly comes from eating too fast and not chewing thoroughly. When we do this, we swallow a lot of air with our food and drink, and this forms a big gas bubble that stretches our stomachs and gives us pain. Also, if we don't chew slowly and thoroughly, the stomach must contract and work harder to churn up the food into small pieces. Hard contractions of the stomach can be painful, too.

Overeating is another cause for stomachache. If we stuff our stomach, it will have to stretch to hold all the food and will have to contract harder to chop it up into small pieces. Sometimes, these hard contractions and the stretching of the muscles of the stomach can give us an awful pain.

If we eat foods that are spoiled or infected with germs, we can get a terrific stomachache, along with nausea and vomiting. Our stomachs are pretty smart organs, and they seem to know when spoiled or poisoned foods are swallowed. It doesn't take long for the stomach to refuse to handle this kind of food, and bingo—the stomach goes into reverse, like an automobile. Then, instead of contracting to push the food further along into the small intestines, the stomach contracts in the opposite direction so that we throw up the rotten food we have accidentally eaten.

We can easily get a stomachache if we eat when we are very upset or ner-

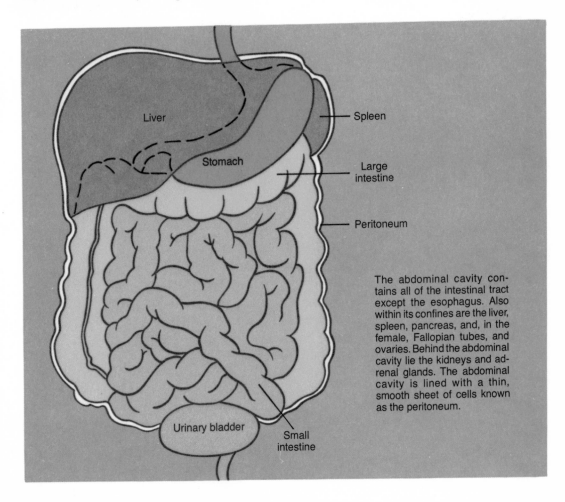

The abdominal cavity contains all of the intestinal tract except the esophagus. Also within its confines are the liver, spleen, pancreas, and, in the female, Fallopian tubes, and ovaries. Behind the abdominal cavity lie the kidneys and adrenal glands. The abdominal cavity is lined with a thin, smooth sheet of cells known as the peritoneum.

vous about something. In order to do its work properly, the stomach must work slowly and steadily. And when we are very unhappy, or very angry, or very sad, the stomach may not work smoothly in churning our food. It may just let the undigested food lie where it is in the stomach, and after a time, this will give us a stomachache. Or, the stomach may contract violently, or in the wrong direction, causing us to throw up.

About one out of ten children has some sort of food allergy. This means that a particular food disagrees with him and may cause the lining of the stomach to be irritated and swollen. When this happens, the stomach will try to get rid of the food by vomiting or by hurrying up its churning so that the food is passed on to the intestines before it is ready to go there. Allergies sometimes cause stomachache because of the violent stomach contractions.

Stomachs can handle proteins and sugars more easily than they can handle fats. But some children, especially overweight ones, like to eat greasy, fried, fatty foods. Then, when they eat too much fat or fried foods, their stomachs rebel and try to get rid of the stuff. Of course, this gives a stomachache.

Once in a while, a child will get an inflammation of the lining of his stomach from a virus. When the lining of the stomach is inflamed, pain can result. In

We can easily get a stomachache if we eat when we are very upset or nervous about something.

addition, the child will probably lose his appetite for a few days.

Gastroenteritis

When the stomach is upset by spoiled or infected food, even though it may have gotten rid of most of it by vomiting, a certain amount of it will pass down into the small intestines. The small intestines act the same way toward this food as the stomach did. They contract very hard and quickly in order to get rid of it. These hard and rapid contractions can cause a very severe pain in the belly. And when the small intestines pass the food on quickly toward the large intestines, the child soon develops loose stools, or diarrhea.

In most cases in which the stomach lining is inflamed by a virus infection, the lining of the small intestines is affected, too. There is a big, long name for this condition. It is called gastroenteritis. Really, all it means is that both the stomach *and* the intestines are affected. But there is no reason to worry; the stomachache and the diarrhea caused by gastroenteritis will last only a few days and will clear up completely.

Constipation

Constipation means that we are unable to move our bowels as often and as completely as we should. It also means that when we do move them, the stool is harder than it ought to be. Most children have a bowel movement once or twice a day, but others only have one every second or third day. And in some cases, constipation can lead to pain in the belly.

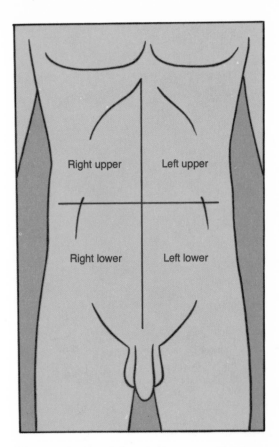

The quadrants of the abdomen are the four regions into which the abdomen may be divided for purposes of physical examination and diagnosis.

Most children who are constipated get that way because they are careless about their bowel habits. Instead of trying to move their bowels at the same time each morning after breakfast, they rush out of the house without going to the bathroom. And, it is often impossible to take the time out of the classroom to have one in school. As a result, they let their movement go until the next day. However, they then discover that it is much more difficult to have a movement the next day as the

107

stool has become very hard. Also, it may be somewhat painful to have a movement when the stool is exceptionally hard. A child who is always constipated soon finds out that he gets frequent pain in his belly, especially when the large intestines try to get rid of the stool.

Inflammation of the appendix

Appendicitis is an inflammation of a little structure attached to the beginning of the large intestine called the appendix. Appendicitis is discussed in the next chapter.

We can't help getting a stomachache once in a while, but there are certain things we can do to avoid getting them too often:

1. Eat slowly and chew thoroughly before swallowing.

2. Do not overeat.

3. Don't eat too many greasy, spicy, fried, or fatty foods.

4. Don't drink too many sodas. The gas in them may give you a stomachache.

5. Don't eat any food that has been lying out in a hot sun for hours, especially salads that have salad dressings.

6. Don't eat too much when you are nervous or upset.

7. Don't eat strange new foods unless your parents tell you it is O.K. to do so.

8. Don't eat anything you think you might be allergic to.

9. Eat very little when you have diarrhea.

10. Go to the bathroom regularly each morning after breakfast to move your bowels.

Eat slowly and chew thoroughly before swallowing.

Appendicitis

Until recently, appendicitis was one of the most common conditions affecting young people. Except for removal of the tonsils, removal of the appendix used to be performed more often than any other operation. However, within the past fifteen to twenty years, inflammation of the appendix doesn't take place so often. Doctors think that the widespread use of the antibiotic medicines has cut down on the power and strength of the germs that used to cause appendicitis. Still, today, in undeveloped countries where they don't have too many antibiotic medications available, appendicitis continues to be extremely common.

Appendicitis usually starts out like an ordinary stomachache, with crampy pains all over the abdominal area. Then, instead of the cramps disappearing by themselves, the patient develops nausea and vomiting. Following this within a few hours, the pain gets worse and travels down to the lower right side of the belly.

The appendix is about as long as a grown-up's little finger and is shaped something like a worm. It is about as thick as a lead pencil. The appendix connects with the large intestine but, so far as we know, it has no function and isn't really needed by our bodies at all.

When the appendix becomes infected, it swells and fills with pus. A child with appendicitis not only will feel pain in the abdomen, but when a doctor examines the area with his

The appendix is about as long as a grownup's little finger, is shaped something like a worm and is about as thick as a lead pencil.

hand, it will feel very tender. Appendicitis causes fever and an increase in the number of white blood cells in the blood. The increased number of white cells helps to fight the germs that have produced the infection.

Because appendicitis often starts out like an ordinary upset stomach, a child is sometimes given a laxative or an enema. These are not good ways of treating appendicitis, and in many

The normal appendix is three to five inches long and pinkish gray with a glistening coat. The inflamed appendix is much thicker, is altered in color, and contains pus.

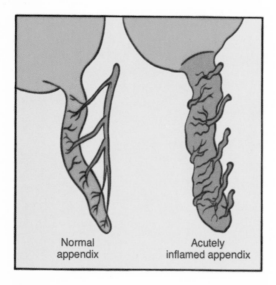

Normal appendix

Acutely inflamed appendix

cases, it makes the condition worse. And so, there is a rule that almost all mothers know: *Never give a child a laxative, an enema, or even food or liquid, when he has a stomachache.*

There are a couple of good ways to tell appendicitis from an ordinary upset stomach. Stomachaches caused by an upset stomach usually clear up by themselves within a few hours, while the pain of appendicitis continues in the belly and often gets worse if something isn't done to treat it. Also, a child with a stomachache caused by an upset stomach will usually develop loose stools and diarrhea, while those with appendicitis are constipated or don't move their bowels at all.

Once a doctor has decided that a child has appendicitis, he will recommend that he go to the hospital. Occasionally, a mild attack of appendicitis

can be treated at home by giving antibiotics, but most cases will require that the appendix be removed by a surgeon in a hospital. It has been discovered that a child who has had one attack of appendicitis, even if it was very mild, will eventually get another attack. Therefore, the sensible thing to do is to remove the appendix with the first attack. Then the child will never have appendicitis again!

The operation for removal of the appendix is called an appendectomy. It is not a very serious operation, unless the condition has been neglected for a day or two. In the ordinary case, the child goes to sleep in the operating room and the appendix is removed in about fifteen to twenty minutes. The cut to remove the appendix is only about two to three inches long and is located in

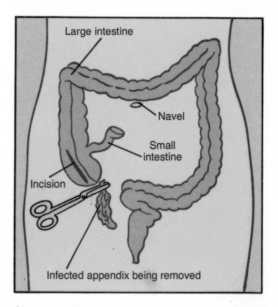

Large intestine

Navel

Small intestine

Incision

Infected appendix being removed

An appendectomy is considered a routine operation in which a structure of no value to the body is removed. There are no problems unless the appendix is ruptured.

the lower right side of the abdomen.

After the operation, the child will have some pain where the incision was made, but in most cases the pain is not severe enough to prevent him from getting out of bed the day after the operation. The appetite may be poor for a few days after the appendix has been removed but it returns to normal within about a week's time.

On the sixth or seventh day after an appendectomy, the stitches are removed. And, if the temperature is normal, in all probability, the child will be able to go home from the hospital.

Some youngsters worry about pain from removing stitches. Actually, it is not very painful at all. It takes less than a minute to cut them, and all a child feels is a slight sticking sensation. Rarely does it cause enough pain for a child to cry.

Children who have had their appendix removed usually stay home from school for about three weeks. This period of time is necessary for the cut to heal solidly. Of course, a child could go back to school earlier, but then he would have to be very careful not to run or play too hard with his classmates. And it isn't always easy to do that, is it?

About two months after the appendix has been taken out, the wound has healed so solidly that children can resume all their activities, such as bicycling, tennis, swimming and diving, dancing, baseball, and all other sports.

After the appendectomy, the child will have some pain where the incision was made, but it's not severe enough to prevent him from getting out of bed the day after the operation.

Bowel Function

By the time a child reaches three to four years of age, he can control his bowels pretty well. Once in a great while, an accident does happen, but that's not a serious matter. It can happen to a grown-up, too. But it is rather important to develop good bowel habits when young, because habits in childhood often continue on into adulthood. And if a child develops good bowel habits, he will probably maintain them as a teenager and grown-up. Also, if he is careless about his bowels as a child, he may remain that way always.

Good bowel habits are:

1. Try to go to the bathroom at the same time each morning. Many children go after breakfast, while others prefer to go before breakfast. Either is all right, if the bowels function properly.

2. Always leave plenty of time for taking care of the bowels. If a child is late for school, he will hurry and may not perform his duties the way he should. This will lead to poor bowel habits.

3. Don't sit on the toilet for longer than necessary. Ten to fifteen minutes should be the limit. Some children like to read while on the toilet. When they do that, they frequently forget why

Don't sit on the toilet for longer than necessary. Some children like to read while on the toilet. When they do that, they frequently forget why they are there.

they are there. It is perhaps best just to do one's job and to get on with the day's activities.

4. Don't strain too hard if it is difficult to move the bowels. Straining can cause a scratch in the delicate tissues in the anal region. If you can't do your business, let your mother know, and she will give you a medicine to make it easier for you.

5. If the bowels are too loose, it is also a good idea to let your mother know. She may give you some medicine to correct the condition. Of course, she will notify your doctor if the loose bowels continue for more than a day or two.

6. Make sure to clean yourself thoroughly before leaving the bathroom. The delicate tissues get irritated very easily if they are unclean. And some irritations in the anal area may last for quite some time and cause a great deal of unpleasant itching.

7. Be sure to wash your hands, too, before leaving the bathroom.

8. Tell your mother if it is very painful to move your bowels. Normally, the process shouldn't be painful. Pain is most often caused by constipation, with very hard stools.

9. Tell your mother if you ever notice blood on the paper. This may mean that there *is* a scratch in the membranes, or it may mean that there is an inflammation of the large intestines or rectum.

Children who neglect their bowels and are irregular about the time each day that they go to the bathroom often become constipated. Constipation is nothing to get excited about when it

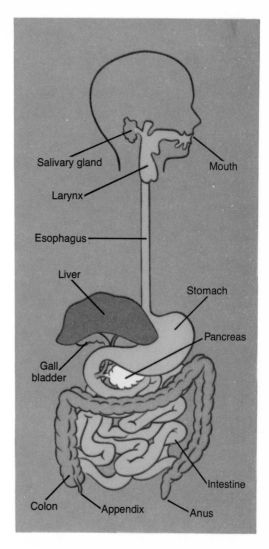

The body's system for absorbing nutrients from food and getting rid of solid waste products begins in the mouth and ends in the bowels. To keep the system in good working order, we must develop regular bowel habits.

happens once in a while, but if a child always finds it difficult to move his bowels, it is a matter for concern. A child who is always constipated may not have as much energy and pep as a

113

child who is regular. Furthermore, children who are constipated sometimes don't have very good appetites, and they may lose valuable weight.

The best treatment for constipation is to drink plenty of water and eat those foods which are most likely to lead to regular movements. These foods include fresh fruit and fruit juices like prune juice and orange and grapefruit juice, plenty of fresh vegetables like lettuce and tomatoes and celery and cabbage and string beans, and plenty of cereals and breads. Foods like whole-wheat bread and cereals contain bran, and bran helps to keep the bowels regular.

If a child is constipated only occasionally, he may be given a laxative or an enema to clear up the condition. However, it is not a good idea to give a child laxatives or enemas regularly. It is a much better idea for the child to develop good bowel habits. That will solve most problems of constipation.

It is not natural for youngsters to have loose stools all the time. (Loose stools mean diarrhea.) If they do, it may mean that their diet is poor and needs to be improved. Perhaps they are getting too few vitamins in their diet, or perhaps they are eating foods to which they are allergic. One child once had diarrhea for many weeks until it was discovered that he had unexpectedly become allergic to milk. When he stopped drinking milk, the loose stools disappeared.

In some instances, diarrhea is caused by an infection or inflammation within the small or large intestine. If this is the cause, a doctor will give medicines to control it.

Any child who has loose stools for more than a day or two should not neglect to tell his or her mother. Diarrhea can be cleared up much more quickly if it is treated early.

Foods that promote regular bowel function are fresh fruits and fruit juices, fresh vegetables, and whole-grain cereals and breads. Whole-wheat breads and cereals contain bran, which is very helpful in keeping the bowels regular.

Doctors used to place a penny or a dime in the opening of the hernia of the belly button, with adhesive tape.

Hernia

A hernia, or as some people call it, a rupture, is a weakness in the wall of the abdomen. It allows intestines or other tissues from inside the abdomen to bulge through the weakened area. The two most frequent places for hernia in children are the bellybutton and the groin. Hernias may also occur at other places, including the diaphragm which separates the chest from the abdomen.

Some children are born with hernias due to a weakness located at the bellybutton, or in the groin where the thigh joins the abdomen. These hernias are thought to be caused by incomplete development of the child in his mother's uterus. In other words, the child was born before he was completely finished.

A hernia in the bellybutton is called an *umbilical hernia*. It is recognized by the way the bellybutton bulges out, especially when an infant cries or strains. Beneath this bulge, one can sometimes feel a little opening in the muscle of the abdominal wall.

Many umbilical hernias get smaller as the child grows during the first year of life, but other umbilical hernias stay the same size or grow larger. If an umbilical hernia is larger than a dime or nickel, and remains that way even after the child has passed his first birthday, it will probably not go away

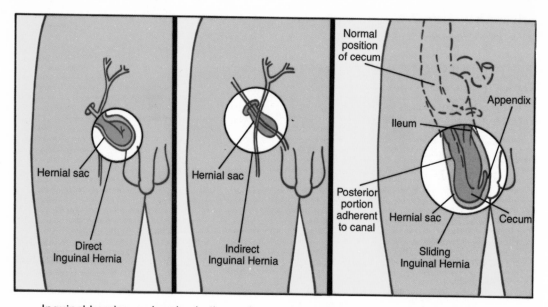

Inguinal hernias, or hernias in the groin, can be very serious if a loop of intestine is caught in the hernial sac. Such hernias should always be repaired surgically. Hernias occur most frequently in the groin, because at this site there are gaps in the abdominal wall for blood vessels and the genital cord.

of its own accord.

Doctors used to place a penny or dime in the opening of a hernia of the bellybutton, would strap it there with adhesive tape, and would leave it in place for several weeks at a time. They thought that this might make the hernia heal by itself. We now know that this doesn't do much good. If an umbilical hernia is going to heal, it will heal even if we leave it alone.

An umbilical hernia can easily be cured by having a surgeon fix it. This is a simple operation, carried out in a hospital. It is not a painful operation because the child goes to sleep before it is performed. Afterward, there might be slight pain for a day or two, but it is not enough to keep the child in bed. Youngsters get out of bed the day after

this type of surgery and they go home from the hospital a day or two later.

A hernia in the groin is called an *inguinal hernia*. Inguinal hernias are just as common as hernias of the bellybutton. When a hernia appears in one groin in a child under one or two years of age, there is a good chance he will develop a hernia in the other groin, too.

Every once in a while an inguinal hernia will clear up by itself by the time a baby reaches the age of a year or a year and a half. However, most of them do not clear up and have to be operated upon.

It is a good idea to operate on inguinal hernias, because there is a tendency for intestines to stick through the bulge of the hernia. When this happens, a child may get sick to his stomach and have pain in his abdomen. And, once in a while, a piece of intestine gets caught in the bulge of the hernia and doesn't go back into the abdomen where it belongs. When this happens a child gets truly sick and must go to the hospital at once.

Most doctors recommend that inguinal hernias be repaired soon after they appear. If they appear at birth, they can be repaired when the child is a few weeks old. If they appear for the first time when a boy or girl is five or six years of age, they are repaired then.

The operation to cure an inguinal hernia is just as simple as the one to fix a hernia of the bellybutton. The child feels no pain during the surgery, as he goes to sleep beforehand. There is some discomfort in the groin for a day or two after the operation, but it doesn't prevent the child from getting out of bed and walking around his hospital room.

About two or three days after repairing an inguinal hernia, the child can go home.

After any operation for hernia, a child must take it easy for a few weeks so that the tissues heal solidly. This means that he may not be able to run and play, to roughhouse or to ride his bicycle for a few weeks. However, he can go back to school just two or three weeks after surgery. When the wound of the operation has healed solidly, he can do everything that he did before he was operated on. The bellybutton and the groin, after a hernia operation, are just as strong as they would have been if no hernia had existed.

Sometimes, in some hospitals, a mother may stay overnight with the child who goes in for a hernia operation. This depends upon the rules of the particular hospital to which the child goes.

A hernia, or as some people call it, a rupture, is a weakness in the wall of the abdomen.

A bladder infection increases the desire to urinate more often.

Kidney and Bladder Infections

The kidneys filter out waste materials and poisons from the blood and get rid of them in the urine. However, sometimes the blood that reaches the kidneys is so full of toxins (poisons manufactured by germs) from a severe inflammation elsewhere in the body that the kidneys themselves become inflamed. For instance, it is possible that a very bad infection of the tonsils may allow a great deal of poisonous toxin to get into the blood and eventually reach the kidneys. And these toxins can be so strong that they cause an inflammation of the kidneys. Also, every once in a while, germs will travel through the blood to the kidneys, where they will cause an infection. And, sometimes, an infection of the bladder may travel up the ureters (the tubes connecting the kidneys and the bladder) and cause a kidney infection.

An inflammation or infection of the kidneys can usually be diagnosed because the child has a high fever, a pain in his back under his ribs where the kidneys are located, and he is tender when the doctor touches the kidneys during his examination. Also, when the doctor examines the urine, he finds pus or other cells which show that the kidneys are inflamed.

In order to get over a kidney inflammation or infection, a child must do the following:

1. Stay in bed.

2. Drink the proper amounts of fluids that the doctor tells him to drink.

3. Take antibiotic medicines or other medicines that the doctor prescribes.

In most cases, a kidney infection will get well without too much trouble, but some of the inflammations caused by toxins may take a long time to get over.

Often, when the kidneys are infected, the bladder also becomes infected. That is quite natural as the urine, containing germs, travels from the kidneys down to the bladder.

It is easy to know when children have bladder infections. Here's what happens in most cases:

1. There is a desire to urinate much more often than usual. Sometimes, a child wants to go every hour, or even more often than that.

2. The urine may burn as it passes out of the body.

3. Even though the child has finished urinating, he or she still feels like doing more.

4. There may be a fever, and the child may perspire a great deal.

5. The urine, instead of being clear, looks cloudy. That's because it contains germs and pus cells.

Luckily, almost all bladder infections can be cleared up quickly if the child stays in bed, drinks large amounts of liquids, and takes the antibiotic medication that the doctor tells him to take. But even after the bladder is all better, it is important to drink lots of water for several weeks afterward. That will prevent the infection from coming back.

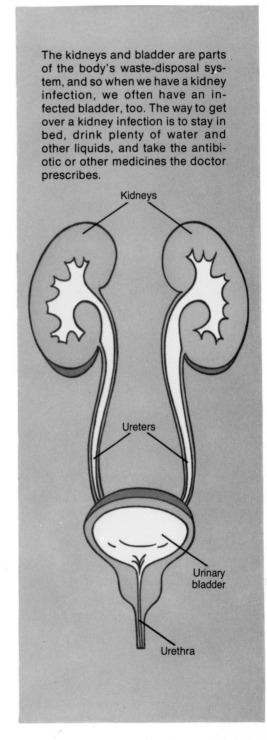

The kidneys and bladder are parts of the body's waste-disposal system, and so when we have a kidney infection, we often have an infected bladder, too. The way to get over a kidney infection is to stay in bed, drink plenty of water and other liquids, and take the antibiotic or other medicines the doctor prescribes.

Kidneys

Ureters

Urinary bladder

Urethra

Don't drink any water in a foreign land unless you are sure it is pure.

NO, THANKS!

Parasites

A parasite is a plant or animal that lives on the outside or inside of another plant or animal. It gets its nourishment from the animal or plant on which, or in which, it lives. Some parasites are so small that they can only be seen under a microscope. For example, the parasite that lives in human blood and causes malaria is so tiny it can only be seen under a microscope. However, some parasites, like the tapeworm which at-

taches itself to the inside of an animal's or human's stomach, may grow to be several feet long.

The world is full of all kinds of parasites. An orchid plant that attaches itself to the bark of a tree is a parasite; many vines are parasites; a tick that attaches itself to a dog's skin and sucks its blood for nourishment is a parasite; and many kinds of worms that get inside an animal's or human's body and

120

gain their nourishment from the animal or human are parasites.

Diseases caused by parasites are fairly common in children who play in dirt where worms and other parasites live. The parasites often go from the ground into a child's body when the child puts his dirty hands into his mouth. Parasites also get into childrens' bodies when they kiss or hug or play with pets who have infected worms or ticks on their bodies. And finally, parasites may enter the body when an infected insect, like a mosquito carrying the malaria parasite, bites someone's skin.

There are a great number of different diseases and conditions caused by parasites. Here are just a few of them, and how they affect children:

Malaria

This is an infection caused by one of four kinds of malarial parasite. It comes about when a person is bitten by a mosquito that is infected with the parasite.

During the first week of malaria, the patient will have attacks of fever, headaches, and chilly sensations. Then, during the weeks afterward, he may feel fine one day, and the next day he may have a high fever and severe chills lasting for a few hours. Then, he will break out in a great sweat. This situation continues with one day high fever and chills, the next day no fever or chills.

The diagnosis of malaria is made by taking a little sample of the patient's blood and examining it under a micro-

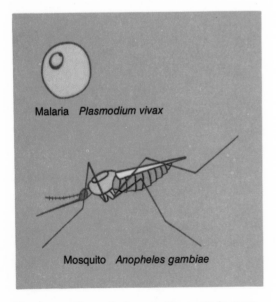

Malaria *Plasmodium vivax*

Mosquito *Anopheles gambiae*

The mosquitoes that carry the malaria parasites breed primarily in the humid, hot climate of the tropics and subtropics. They are seldom found in temperate regions.

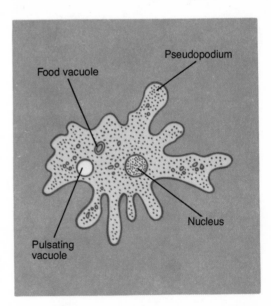

Food vacuole

Pseudopodium

Nucleus

Pulsating vacuole

An ameba is a single-celled animal organism that may cause diseases in children. The most common of such diseases is dysentery caused by Endamoeba histolytica.

121

scope. On examination, the malaria parasite will be found.

Malaria attacks may go on for many weeks or months if treatment isn't given. Fortunately, there are several excellent medications to control malaria, but they must be given over a long period of time in order to cure the condition.

To prevent this disease, someone

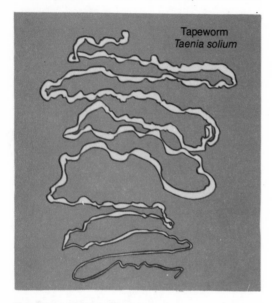

Tapeworm
Taenia solium

Tapeworms sometimes grow to be many feet long. Medicines may cause the worm to be passed out of the intestines. Unless the head of the worm comes out with the segments, the worm will continue to grow.

who is in an area where malaria exists should take antimalarial pills every day. Also, he should protect himself against being bitten by mosquitoes.

Amebic dysentery

This is a form of diarrhea caused by a tiny one-celled animal parasite called the ameba. A child with amebic dysentery will have crampy pains in his ab-

domen, many watery, loose bowel movements, loss of appetite, loss of weight, and anemia.

The diagnosis of this condition is made by examining the stool in a laboratory and seeing the ameba parasite under a microscope.

Luckily, there are excellent medicines to kill the parasite and cure the child.

To prevent amebic dysentery, a child must be very clean about his body and his eating habits. Also, if he isn't careful, he may spread the infection to other members of his family.

Worms

Various worms can easily get into a child's body if he runs barefoot outdoors, if he has the habit of putting dirty fingers into his mouth, or if he plays with animals who have worms.

There are dozens of different kinds of worms, including the hookworm, the whipworm, the pinworm, and the tapeworm. Each one can get into the body, and each one can cause a different disease.

Some of the worms that get into the stomach and intestines finally come out in the stool. When they appear in the stool, doctors can examine them and will therefore be able to tell the exact kind of worm that is causing trouble. Occasionally, a worm will get into the blood, or will reach the muscles or other organs of the body. These worms may be harder to find, but there are ways of discovering and getting rid of them.

People are fortunate that doctors have discovered medicines to kill prac-

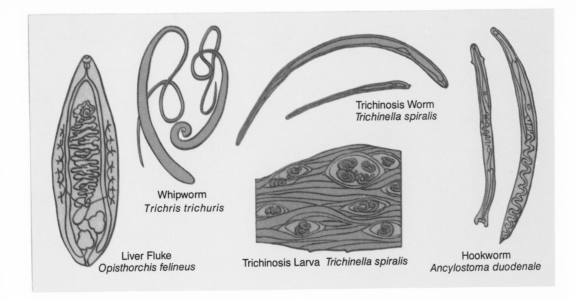

Whipworm
Trichris trichuris

Trichinosis Worm
Trichinella spiralis

Liver Fluke
Opisthorchis felineus

Trichinosis Larva *Trichinella spiralis*

Hookworm
Ancylostoma duodenale

Among the parasites found in children are: whipworm, hookworm, trichinosis larva in muscle, adult trichinosis worm, and liver fluke.

tically every type of worm that can get into the body.

Precautions

Here are some good rules to follow if we want to avoid conditions caused by parasites:

1. Don't drink any water in the country or in a foreign land unless you are positive it is pure. Don't eat the skins of raw fruits and raw vegetables when you are visiting in the country. Fresh fruit should be peeled, and raw vegetables should be cooked.

2. Children should protect themselves against mosquitoes, and against lice and other insects that might carry parasites. Mosquito sprays should be used. Long slacks or jeans, long-sleeved blouses or shirts, should be worn in areas where there are mosquitoes.

3. Vaccinations should be given against diseases carried by insects and viruses. For example, before traveling to some foreign countries, it is a good idea to be vaccinated against typhus fever, yellow fever, the plague, and other contagious diseases. When going to an area where there is malaria, a child should take antimalarial pills every day. And when camping out in woods where there might be ticks, it might be wise to be vaccinated against Rocky Mountain spotted fever.

4. Children should not kiss and hug dogs or cats or other pets that run wild in the fields. Such animals may carry insects that can transmit parasites.

5. Children should wash thoroughly when they come indoors and, of course, they should never put dirty fingers in their mouths!

123

Birthmarks, Moles, and Warts

Someday doctors will probably have a vaccine that is effective in preventing warts.

Many infants are born with some kind of birthmark or mole somewhere on their bodies. They may appear as a light pinkish spot on the face, neck, or torso, or they may be a coffee-colored mark. Occasionally, a child is born with a deeper red wine-stain birthmark. Unfortunately, many of these wine-stain marks are found on the face or head where sometimes they don't look very nice.

Some birthmarks are pretty difficult to get rid of, but actually, most of them don't need to be gotten rid of because they aren't disfiguring. Birthmarks don't cause any pain and the ones on covered parts of the body can't even be seen unless one is undressed.

Many light-colored pink birthmarks fade out and disappear by themselves before the child is a few months old. Ugly-looking, darker-colored birthmarks on the face can often be removed by a surgeon when the child has grown up a bit and is better able to undergo an operation.

A great many boys and girls will develop a mole or two by the time they reach five or six years of age. Moles are round in shape and are raised slightly from the surface of the skin. Some are light tan while others are a deeper-brown or even a bluish-black color. Moles can be as small as a pinhead or may be extremely large, occasionally reaching the size of a lemon or orange. Children with many moles usually have a mother or father, or both, who also have a lot of moles on their bodies.

Moles that aren't ugly or disfiguring can be left alone unless they begin to grow rapidly or change from a lighter to a darker color, or bleed because they are rubbed against by clothing. It is also a good idea to remove moles that was removed.

Almost every child sooner or later will have a wart. Warts are caused by a virus infection. There used to be a story that warts came from playing with frogs or toads, but we now know that this just isn't true. Warts are round and hard and raised above the surface of the skin. The top of a wart feels rough and horny.

Warts can appear anywhere on the body, but favorite places are on the hands and feet. It is not known why some youngsters have lots of warts and others have practically none. Doctors

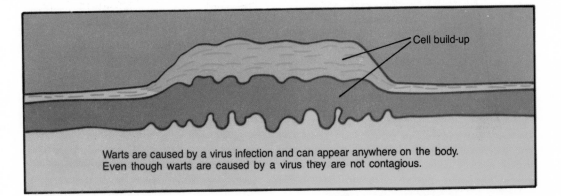

Cell build-up

Warts are caused by a virus infection and can appear anywhere on the body. Even though warts are caused by a virus they are not contagious.

are on the toes or feet or fingers or hands, because they often get irritated. To have a mole removed, a child usually goes to the hospital for a day. Most moles can be removed very easily, either with a little injection to relieve the pain or by getting an anesthetic so as to go to sleep during the operation. Operations to remove moles are not painful and children don't mind the experience very much at all. If a mole happens to be especially ugly, the scar following its removal will look much better than the mole looked before it

think that certain children just naturally seem better able than others to protect themselves against the viruses that cause warts.

Often, warts will last for a few weeks or months, and then, with nothing done about them, they disappear. Other times, warts do not go away, or they may grow larger and the child may develop more of them in the same or a different part of the body. And, sometimes, a doctor will remove just one wart, and all the rest of them will disappear all by themselves.

If warts are painful, as they often are when located on the sole of the foot, they should be treated. Also, warts that are large and ugly, and those that are constantly being irritated by shoes or clothing, should be removed. There are several ways of treating warts. Here are some of them:

1. They can be scraped away with a special instrument called a curette.

2. They can be burned away with an electric needle. This is kind of painful to do, but the doctor will relieve the pain by giving an injection of a local anesthetic before he starts to burn the wart.

3. They can be destroyed by placing a special acid on them.

4. X-ray treatment can be given to make them disappear.

5. A surgeon can cut out a wart with a scalpel (surgeon's knife).

There isn't much a child can do to avoid warts. Parents used to think that cleanliness would prevent warts, but this doesn't seem to be true in all cases. Of course, children who aren't clean are more likely to get any kind of infection more often than clean youngsters, and this goes for warts, too. So far, doctors don't have a vaccine that is effective in preventing warts but, some day, they probably will have a vaccine that will work for this condition.

Even though warts are caused by a virus, they aren't contagious. In other words, if you play with a child who has warts, you won't catch them from him.

There used to be a story that warts came from playing with frogs or toads . . .

. . . but we know now that this just isn't true.

Going to the Hospital

Friends and relatives can visit patients every day during visiting hours.

Hospitals are fine places, because that's where sick people go to get better. Without them, it would be much more difficult for doctors to cure their patients. And there is another reason why hospitals are great. Do you know what that is? Well, it's where your mom went to have you!

Sooner or later, almost everybody goes to a hospital for some reason or other. Maybe it's to have tonsils removed, or to have an appendix out, or to have tests done for a sickness that isn't getting well quickly enough at home, or to have a broken arm or leg fixed. The fact is that hospitals have the equipment and the instruments and the machines and the medicines and the special doctors to cure most diseases. A doctor's office can't have all that equipment or medicines or different kinds of specialists. And certainly, your home doesn't have an X-ray machine and a laboratory to do blood tests, or an operating room, does it?

The main trouble with hospitals is that many of them won't let your mom or dad stay overnight with you when you are there. Some might allow this,

Although a child is likely to be at least a little homesick and anxious for a day or two after entering the hospital, he will soon meet other children and enjoy the recreational and entertainment programs that many hospitals provide.

but many hospitals don't. And, of course, no youngster likes the idea of being separated from his parents. But it can't be helped sometimes, and most children realize that they are only going to be in the hospital a short time, so it won't make too much difference.

To make up for your parents not being with you, many hospitals have specially developed programs to entertain children. In some hospitals, it's pretty much like being in a play group in school. There are special sections of the hospital set aside for children so that they will have plenty of friends to play with. And hospitals have books for the children to read and games and toys to play with. Some hospitals even have shows and movies for the children. That sounds pretty good, doesn't it?

Would you like to know what happens to children when they go to the hospital? Here goes:

1. A child takes a pair or two of pajamas or nightgowns, and a bathrobe and slippers to the hospital as well as a comb and brush, and toothbrush and toothpaste.

It isn't necessary to take a radio or

television as they have them available in the hospital. It is also unnecessary to take toys or games or blankets or pillows. They have those in the hospital, too. A favorite book or two can be brought along, if one wants to.

2. When he gets to the hospital, the child and his or her parents will go to the Admitting Office. There, the mother or father tells the people the child's name, age, and address. They then put this information on a bracelet which is slipped on to the child's wrist. Doing this allows all the nurses and doctors to know exactly who the child is. All they have to do is read the information on the bracelet.

3. From the Admitting Office, the child goes to his room. It may have only one bed, or there may be two, three, four or more beds in the room. It is frequently more fun to be in a room with other youngsters with whom a child can talk and play.

4. After getting to the hospital room, a child undresses and gets into bed. A whole bunch of tests are carried out on almost all patients, no matter what is wrong with them. Here are some of the things that most children experience.

a.) An examination is done by a doctor. Often, the doctor is an intern or resident, and wears a white uniform. It may be a man or a woman doctor.

b.) The nurse takes the child's pulse and temperature.

c.) A laboratory technician takes some blood from the child's finger or arm to send to the laboratory. (This hurts just about as much as a mosquito bite.)

d.) The nurse asks the child to urinate in a bottle so that the urine can be sent to the laboratory for examination.

e.) An X ray of the chest is taken.

The main trouble with hospitals is that many of them won't let your mom and dad stay overnight with you when you are there.

(This doesn't hurt at all.)

f.) Special tests are done, according to the child's illness.

g.) If the child is going to have an operation performed, the skin is shaved in the area that is to be operated upon.

h.) A child who is going to be operated on the next morning may be given an enema the night before. Also, one who is to be operated on the next morning should not eat or drink anything after going to sleep at night.

5. Parents are always allowed to visit their children every day, even if they aren't permitted to stay overnight. They will come each day and will stay during the visiting hours.

Children must understand that it is sometimes not possible for the parents to stay all day long. If they did, the doctors and nurses might not be able to give all the treatments that the sick children require.

6. As soon as a doctor can tell when a child is well enough to go home, the child will be told. It is perfectly all right for a child to ask the doctor when that time will come, but a child must understand that the doctor cannot always tell for sure. Some illnesses clear up in a few days; some take much longer. And, of course, a doctor is not going to send a child home until he is completely recovered.

7. The best way to go home quickly is for children to cooperate fully with their doctors and nurses. If they take their medicines and treatments without raising a fuss, they will get well much more quickly.

A parent can help prepare a young child for a visit to the hospital by reading the child picture books about hospitals and talking about them in a general way.

*Everyone in the operating room
must wear a cap and a face mask
that covers the nose and mouth.*

Anesthesia and Surgery

It doesn't hurt to be operated upon because one goes to sleep and feels no pain while the surgeon is doing what he has to do. No matter what the operation, whether it is the removal of tonsils or the appendix, or the fixing of a hernia, pain is never felt. Oh, there may be a little pain when a patient awakens from the operation, but most of that pain, too, can be gotten rid of by giving special pain-relieving medicines.

The word anesthesia means absence of feeling. There are lots of ways to see to it that the patient feels nothing during an operation. Some of them are:

1. Giving special medicines an hour or so before the operation while the patient is still in his hospital bed.

2. Giving an injection of a medicine that makes the patient go to sleep on the operating table in the operating room.

3. Giving the patient an anesthetic gas to breathe.

There are several different gases that can put a person completely to sleep, unable to feel pain. Here are the names of some of them: fluothane; cyclopropane; nitrous oxide; ether; ethyl chloride.

These gases are breathed in through a special anesthesia mask that is attached by a rubber tube to an anesthesia machine that contains tanks of the gases. And, as we have mentioned before, the gases are given only after the patient has been placed in a nice, relaxed state by medicine received even before being brought to the operating room. The doctor who specializes in anesthesia will choose the gas he or she thinks best for the particular patient and the particular operation the surgeon is going to perform.

Here is what usually happens when a child goes, with his or her mother or father, of course, to the hospital for an operation:

1. The day before the operation the anesthesiologist (the doctor who specializes in anesthesia) visits the child in the hospital room and explains everything that is going to happen about anesthesia.

2. Anesthesiologists often show the patient the anesthesia mask that will be used in giving the anesthetic the next day. A child might want to practice breathing through it, even though it is not attached to an anesthesia machine.

3. An enema may be given the night

Before the operation the surgeon or anesthesiologist visits a young patient, makes friends with her, and explains how anesthesia will be administered to her.

The morning of the operation, the patient is given a special shirt to wear in the operating room.

before the operation so the stomach and intestines will be empty. That often does away with any uncomfortable feeling in the belly after the operation is over.

4. No food or drink is given to the patient after the evening meal in the hospital the night before the operation. This will keep the stomach nice and empty so one won't feel sick to the stomach after the operation is over.

5. A sleeping pill, or even an injection, may be given the night before, just to make sure the patient has a good sleep and isn't restless the next morning before going to the operating room.

6. A special medicine is injected an hour or so before going to the operating room in the morning. This makes certain the patient feels relaxed and comfortable when given the anesthetic gas to breathe.

7. The morning of the operation, the patient is given a special shirt to wear to the operating room. After the operation, the patient will put on his or her own pajamas or nightgown again.

8. To travel to the operating room, a patient is put on a special stretcher. A child says goodbye to mother and father, but will see them again soon after waking up after the operation.

9. The operating room is usually on a different floor—called the surgical

floor—in the hospital from the patient's room. This may mean a ride, while on the stretcher, in an elevator.

10. Upon reaching the surgical floor, the patient will again greet the anesthesiologist. Together, they will go into the operating room, and the child will move off the stretcher to the operating table.

11. The patient lies back on the operating table and, looking up, can see a huge light. This operating light is very special because it throws a very strong beam without any shadows. This permits the surgeon and aides to see perfectly what they are doing. Many children like to ask to see the light turned on before they go to sleep.

12. The surgeon who is going to do the operation comes in and greets the patient.

13. The patient will notice that there are quite a few people who were not around before, hustling and bustling about the operating room. These are:

a.) The instrument nurse who is handling a bunch of surgical instruments. She will assist at the operation.

b.) The circulating nurse. She's the one who comes in and out of the operating room to bring the instrument nurse various things she needs.

c.) An orderly. He is a man who helps to keep the operating room neat and clean in between operations. He may be the same man who brought the patient from his room to the operating room, and he may be the one who lifts the patient onto the operating table before the operation and lifts him off after the operation.

d.) There may be one or two doctors other than the patient's surgeon in the operating room. They are there to assist the surgeon perform the operation.

14. Everyone in the operating room wears a cap, a face mask covering the nose and mouth, and a special gown that is put on backwards. The cap, mask, and gown are worn in order to keep everything as free as possible from germs. Of course, everybody knows that things should be germ-free (sterile) in an operating room. This will keep germs away from the surgical

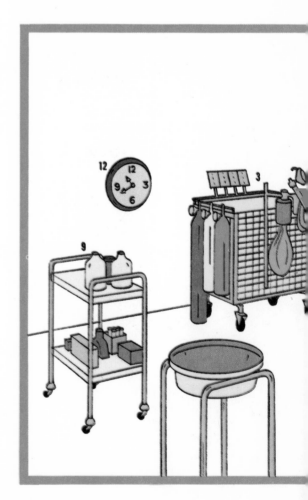

134

wound so that it will heal quickly, without infection.

15. The surgeon and surgical assistants, at about this time, leave the operating room and go to scrub sinks. These are specially designed sinks where the surgeons scrub their hands and arms with special brushes or sponges. They scrub and scrub for about ten minutes without stopping. This gets the germs off their hands and arms so they can't get into the surgical incision.

16. While the surgeons are scrubbing, and before they have put on their operating gowns and rubber gloves, the anesthesiologist starts putting the patient to sleep. First, he or she gives an injection into the hand or arm and attaches the needle to a plastic bag containing fluid. This fluid has sugar in it so the patient will receive nourishment even while the operation is going on. Then the anesthesiologist takes the anesthesia mask and gently places it over the patient's nose and mouth.

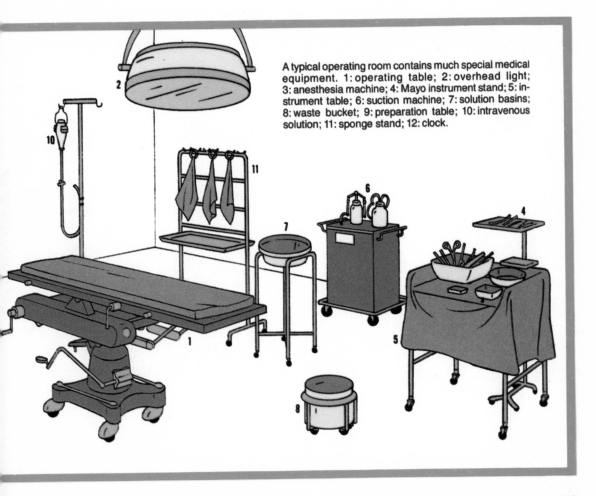

A typical operating room contains much special medical equipment. 1: operating table; 2: overhead light; 3: anesthesia machine; 4: Mayo instrument stand; 5: instrument table; 6: suction machine; 7: solution basins; 8: waste bucket; 9: preparation table; 10: intravenous solution; 11: sponge stand; 12: clock.

It is no wonder so many youngsters just can't wait to tell their friends about their operations!

The patient takes a few deep breaths and—almost quick as a wink—falls asleep. And, of course, the patient stays asleep until the operation is finished.

17. A patient waking up from an operation may feel some pain in the wound area, but is still so groggy from the anesthesia that the pain won't be remembered. Most patients doze off and on for an hour or two after the operation has been completed. This is O.K. Everybody will let them sleep. A patient may also feel thirsty, but it is usually a good idea not to drink anything for an hour or two after surgery. Drinking might make the patient sick to the stomach.

18. From the operating room, patients are brought to the recovery room, which is near the operating room. There are special recovery-room nurses who know all the ways to make someone who has just undergone surgery feel comfortable. If pain is severe, they will give medicines to relieve it. If the patient is sweaty, the nurses will sponge him or her off. Finally, when the patient has fully awakened, another ride on a stretcher brings a return to his or her own hospital room. A child, of course, will be greeted there by one or both parents.

There may be a few uncomfortable hours even after a child is back in the hospital room after an operation. But most children sleep a lot and don't complain too much. Do you know why? Well, it's because they are so happy the operation is over.

Most patients get out of bed the morning after an operation. Some can go home the day following surgery;

136

others must wait longer, until the wound has healed. When the wound has healed, maybe six or seven days later, the surgeon will remove the stitches. However, in certain types of cases it is possible to put in stitches that absorb by themselves and don't have to be removed. But if these kinds have not been used, a patient should know that there isn't much pain to removing stitches. There might be a slight pinching feeling as the stitches are removed, but certainly, no more pain than a little mosquito bite.

When children come home after an operation, they begin to realize what a wonderful experience they have had. Just think of it, having your tonsils or appendix removed, and all you remember is going to the operating room on a stretcher and seeing the big light overhead on the operating table! We'll bet you don't even remember the anesthesiologist putting the mask on your face, do you? That's pretty terrific, isn't it? No wonder so many youngsters just can't wait to tell their friends about their operation!

After it's all over, children enjoy showing off their surgical scars. They get attention and have an opportunity to display their bravery to others.

INDEX

Spleen, 67
Sprains, 79, 82, 85
Staphylococcus organisms, 64, *illus.* 64
Stitches, 56, 111, 137
Stomachaches, 104, 108
Streptococcus organisms, *illus.* 30, 48, *illus.* 48, 64, *illus.* 64
Surgery *SEE* Operations

T

Tapeworms, *illus.* 122
Temperatures, 11-13
Tendons, 79, 85
Tetanus shots, 57
Thermometers, 11, *illus.* 12, 13
Throats
   sore throats, 14-15, 47-50
Tiredness, 15, 65
Tonsils, 38, 43-44, *illus.* 44, 48, 94
Trichinosis larva and worms, *illus.* 123

U

Umbilical hernias, 115-116
Urination, 119

V

Vaccinations, 21, 22, 26, 28, *illus.* 29, 30, 96, 98, 123
Ventilation, 15
Vomiting, 17, 19

W

Warts, 125-126, *illus.* 125
Wax in the ears, 41-42, *illus.* 42
Whipworms, *illus.* 123
Whooping cough, 22, 24-25, 26-27
Worms, 122-123, *illus.* 122, *illus.* 123

Y

Yellow jackets, *illus.* 71

ACKNOWLEDGMENTS

The idea for these books evolved during a delightful dinner party attended by members of the Disney organization and the author. The brainstorming began sketchily with hors d'oeuvre but by the time dessert had been served GROWING UP HEALTHY was well on toward its launching. To the very creative Vincent H. Jefferds of Disney, and to his most able associate Don MacLaughlin, our thanks. Our appreciation, too, to Jeanette Kroger for her excellent editorial assistance and to Al White and his wonderful staff of artists.

As with so many of the author's previous works, the advice and encouragement of Harry N. Abrams played an invaluable role in seeing the project through to completion. Also, the author benefited greatly from the helpfulness of Robert Clarke and James Hinkley of Grolier Enterprises. To them, he wishes to express his sincere gratitude.

The author acknowledges the great help he has received from his assistant, Eileen F. Kessler, who spent long hours beyond the call of duty collating material and putting the manuscript into shape for publication.

It gives the author pleasure to record his debt to his son Robert, who suggested several important topics for inclusion in these books. And, finally, the author is in debt to Andrew B. Kay, aged 6 years, who not only gave ideas for topics in *How We Behave* but who listened attentively to much of the manuscript with the friendly, tolerant ear of a grandson.

R.E.R.